Lending a Hand,
Seeing the World

Lending a Hand, Seeing the World

Memoir of an International Volunteer

JUDITH LOVE SCHWAB

Jefferson, North Carolina

All photographs belong to the author unless otherwise noted.

Library of Congress and British Library
Cataloguing data are available

ISBN (print) 978-1-4766-8139-9 ∞
ISBN (ebook) 978-1-4766-4049-5

Front cover images *from top left to right* Ruins in Philippi (photograph by
Ellen Westbrook); Country house and yard (photograph provided
by Patty Carlson Volunteer Relations Manager, Global Volunteers);
Rapa Nui beach (photograph by Louise Jones-Takata); JLS taking notes
in an Italian olive grove (photograph by W. E. Schwab); Anakena,
a white coral sand beach in the Rapa Nui National Park (photograph by
Louise Jones-Takata); Meerkats scramble up anything to look for danger;
Weeding at the Forestry department, (photograph by Louise Jones-Takata)

Printed in the United States of America

Toplight is an imprint of McFarland & Company, Inc., Publishers

*Box 611, Jefferson, North Carolina 28640
www.toplightbooks.com*

For Wally, who kissed me and missed me
and encouraged me to go.

Acknowledgments

Words don't pile up into a book without encouragement and faith from others. My husband, Walter Schwab, admires what I do and has for more than half a century. My Aunt Colleen loved my travel stories so much she said she felt she had gone on those trips with me. From the professional side, I am grateful to Jack Chamberlain, my first editor at *The Roanoke Times,* who taught me to assume nothing and to always get the dog's name. And to Beth Obenshain, Jack's boss, for admiring my work, and to Jo Chamberlain, Jack's wife, who suggested I could be a reporter in the first place.

Thanks also to careful and thoughtful readers: to my friend author Angie Smibert, who advised and supported from her busy desk in Virginia; to mutual friend Susan Bixler, who gave it a careful read; and to poet, writer and teacher Jim McKean and his workshop members at Tinker Mountain Writers' Workshop at Hollins University in Virginia, who commented on an early draft. And a special thanks to Jeff Johnson who heard my book idea the night I met him and suggested I propose my book to his publisher.

Table of Contents

Preface

My family liked to talk and told stories about their adventures and other people's as well, so it was what I did when I came home from a trip. The early ones with family still have versions in the memories of the few older folks who are left. But these stories are not just about where I went and what I did there. This book covers what it took to finally get me on the road without the convenience of another person making the arrangements and inviting me. After my first trip abroad to Poland, where I felt so at home, I naturally wanted to return. When I discovered volunteer vacations, I saw a way to go back to Poland on my own and also to join up with other travelers and do something in one area, thereby sinking into a culture in a way a tour could not provide. That was the beginning of more than twenty years of seeing the world through volunteering.

As a writer, I took notes when I traveled, and then I wrote about the trip when I got home. When people asked about what I did, I could offer stories and pictures. When the Internet and e-mail came along, I began to send out my "trip reports" to those interested. Readers seemed intrigued and said they enjoyed my stories. The reports piled up, and so did the questions: wasn't I scared, lonely? Comments piled up too: I could never do that; I can't believe you were robbed; I would just sit down and cry. Those questions and comments, all from women, made me realize some women felt held back. There were a lot of "what ifs."

In the end, I realized that my feelings about risk are tempered by what I have read in the *Tao Te Ching*. Simply put, when good things happen, good. When bad things happen, good. All this means is that our lives change all the time, as change is the only constant. You can drive to the store for a loaf of bread and break your leg when you slip on a fruit skin in the produce department. "Not good," you say. But perhaps the broken leg keeps you from attending an event during which everyone is exposed to bad food and ends up in the hospital and dangerously ill. Then the broken leg is a good outcome. There is no good. There is no bad. There just is. The trick is to cope with whatever comes along.

I wrote *Lending a Hand, Seeing the World* to entertain those who enjoy travel stories from the comfort of their favorite reading chairs and for those who have considered going out to see the world but have felt held back.

Suitcase pre-trip. My cat, Sally, hoping I won't leave.

Introduction:
How the Travel Seeds
Were Planted and Nourished

The First Trip

It was 1950. My mother sat in the living room with a road map open on her lap. She was carefully tracing a route between where we lived in Pennsylvania to Niagara Falls in Canada. She was using a glass Mercurochrome wand and leaving a rusty, transparent trail over the roads we would take. The color matched the spots on my banged-up knees. I was seven years old, and summer shorts revealed the minor wounds I collected from playing in the woods. Mom was inventing the concept of the highlighter 13 years before the appearance of the actual product while planning a trip that would take us farther than we had ever been before.

The Mercurochrome Trail would be my first trip. My mother worked in a factory every day, making parts for radio tubes and other electronics. One day, she started having what she called "crying jags." The family doctor prescribed, not a pill, not snapping out of it, but rather, a vacation. This was a new concept for our family. My dad, a farmer, couldn't get away, but my mother had vacation time. We lived in a little house with a single cold-water tap in the kitchen, a wood cookstove, and an outhouse out back to save money for the real house my father was building. It was a frugal existence, and vacations had little to do with my parents' experience. But my mother, always the adventurer, created one. First, she needed a car, as we only had the pick-up, and Dad needed it. No problem, my Uncle Joe was conveniently away in Korea fighting a war or taking part in a police action, depending on your point of view. He had gone off as a soldier in the U.S. Army at the request of President Truman and had left his brand new, special ordered, 1949 maroon Chevy club coupe at home. His wife (my father's sister) had just learned to drive it—my mother had taught her. We wouldn't want to leave Grandma and Grandpap home alone, and of course, my aunt's six-month-old baby had to go. So, with the orange route carefully plotted and my little suitcase packed, my dad dropped us at my grandparents' house where my aunt and her baby were living while Uncle Joe was serving his country. Dad helped us pack the trunk, and then we all squeezed in through the two doors and set off.

As we drove each day, the summer air poured through those little triangular vents in the front seat windows to cool us, but by afternoon, heat piled up around us. My mother and her sister-in-law knew they were finished driving for the day (neither grandparent drove) when my otherwise silent grandfather began to read signs aloud. "Eat," then a few more miles, "Café," and then finally, "Beer." The magic combination was food, beer, and a place to sleep for the night. We would find a place with a "Vacancy" sign hung out front, crunch onto the gravel parking lot and get out. The luggage and the camp stove would be hefted from the trunk, and we would proceed to our rental cabin, leaving the Chevy to tick its way cool. Ubiquitous metal lawn chairs with shell-shaped backs flanked the door. Without air conditioning (just like home), the wood doors would sometimes stick from the moisture of the woodsy climate. That's when Grandma would bark, "Bill, open this door," and Grandpap, still as strong as when he was a doughboy Marine in World War I, would put his shoulder to the door. One way or another, that door opened.

Inside the cabin, beds would be claimed, and bottles of beer opened for the grandparents with what was called a church key. Too young for irony, this confused me no end. Then we settled in for a relaxing evening without television. The grownups could play cards. I chased lightning bugs and smacked mosquitoes, and we talked or read. There was no television at home or on the road, and if there was a phone, we didn't want long distance charges, so we didn't use it. In the morning, Grandma, clutching her cotton housecoat tightly around her,

At a tourist cabin. Left to right: My grandmother, Bertha Love, wearing my cowboy hat. Me, wearing my mother's hat. Grandpap, Bill Love, wearing his own hat. My aunt, Colleen Salome, watching from the cabin doorway.

aluminum curlers pinching her skimpy hair, stood outside at the picnic table and cooked breakfast—bacon and eggs, fried bread, and coffee.

At Niagara Falls, we crossed over into Canada, and that was the first time I left the country. I remember the tremendous roaring of the water and the mist forming rainbows. My mother bought me a souvenir book about the falls. I added it to my collection of comic books to read in the back seat, and it became a favorite because it contained two mesmerizing images. One was a drawing of an Indian maiden, "The Maid of the Mist," with cleavage peeping from her buckskin dress. I wondered if I would have that someday, as I peered down my shirt at the two matching pink dots on my washboard chest. The other was a photo of a real mummy found at the site. He or she had a blue face and a smattering of teeth. The entire person was all crisscrossed with rag strips in a sort of bundle. Sex and death, the very subjects everyone hid from me. Travel was terrific.

Except for the incident with U.S. Customs on the way back, the trip was a success. At seven, I had a strong sense of following the rules,

5

The author, age seven, on her first international trip to Niagara Falls, Canada, 1950.

and we were supposed to tell that man in the uniform about the things we bought. Saying very little throughout the trip, I now spoke up and insisted we hadn't shown him "the big thing" my mother had bought me. The adults were confounded. What big thing? The officer was interested. That prompted a car search for my precious felt pennant that we were taking home for my bedroom wall. It seemed big to me.

Back home, my father soon figured out how to hit the road in the truck, while the grandparents stayed home to take care of the farm. It was two years later that he built a wood frame for the bed of the truck and had a canvas maker create a zippered shell. It was rainproof and had plastic windows and rolled up at the sides, a precursor to the hard-shell camper tops to come along later. While Dad was putting in the finishing touches—a double bed mattress and a wood shelf across the back—I made the blank book my mother suggested I take to keep a log of our adventures. I decorated the cover with a drawing of the truck with a line of laundry flying in the breeze behind it, snow-capped mountains in the distance. Then we packed up, Mom, Dad, my mother's youngest sister and me, and headed to Texas to visit family. The adults rode up front, and I bounced my way from Pennsylvania to Texas and back, lying on the mattress or looking out the sides and back or, once again, reading. We camped in state parks with my dad outside on a cot, the women in the back, and me on the front seat. Sometimes, we stayed at motels.

We learned the desert was as hot as everyone said it was, and that water froze overnight in summer in the Rocky Mountains. The old Studebaker made it up Pike's Peak and passed Buicks and Cadillacs with steaming radiators by the side of the road, canvas bags of water looped over their big grille talons. Dad was really proud of that old truck. In order to picnic at White Sands National Monument, in New Mexico, we had to cool our heels in the visitors' area while they tested a rocket. After we spent what seemed like ages inside a building decorated with hand woven Indian rugs and old saddles, we were given the go ahead for the picnic site. The place is the world's largest outcropping of pure gypsum and the largest military installation in the U.S. It was the nineteen fifties, everything was safe, and certainly there was no danger in being near a launch site—the government told us so.

Souvenirs were often honest-to-God pieces of the landscapes. From New Mexico, my mother brought back a container of that gypsum, and it may still be in the house where I grew up. I often wondered what a Geiger counter would have to say near that container. We stopped at the Petrified Forest National Park, an area we thought might have standing, cool rocks and maybe some trees. Instead, it had, well, petrified wood, some in the shape of logs, but mostly lots and lots of small colorful stones. Absolutely no one was around, and it seemed as if we could see in all directions to the curvature of the earth. Then a Park Ranger popped up from nowhere, like the roadrunner in the cartoons. He hustled out to kindly tell us we were not supposed to have gone through the puny barbed wire fence. Hadn't we seen the tiny, rusted, bullet-riddled sign? And we certainly were not allowed to keep the little collection of petrified tree parts we had been stuffing into our pockets.

On that trip, we dipped into Mexico on a day trip. I had officially left the country twice. I wrote in the book I had made—and then lost it, found it, lost it through the years. This book turned out to be the beginning of writing down what I saw and did on my travels. Looking back on those two trips and my life then, I can see how I learned to get along with a minimum of creature comforts when I'm on the road. The shack and our frugality taught me to get by with whatever I had and be happy when more was provided. The heated floors, indoor plumbing, and dishwasher in the new house were worth every previous winter walk to the outhouse. The early trips taught me what I needed to ride in coach so many years later. Sitting on the floor of that Chevy, squeezed against my grandmother's legs, maybe a pop bottle or shoe under the seat, I happily read my comics. As long as I have something to read, something to write with, and a little stash of soap to wash out the quick-to-dry stuff, I'm set.

Early Flying Adventures

I rambled around with the family until I grew up. In college, I so wanted to travel—instead of settling into the daily rat race that was waiting for me as a high school English teacher after graduation—that I signed up for the Peace Corps. This agency had begun the year I graduated from high school. Recruiters came to campus, and I was intrigued. The Peace Corps could be my free ride, literally. I took their exams, which were like college entrance exams, with additional parts testing the ability to learn a foreign language. In retrospect, I realize I never balked at going off and being a volunteer for two years. Like anything learned at your mother's knee, you don't even realize you learned it. After work and school hours or on weekends, she took me with her when she delivered a cake, a pie, or deviled eggs—or flowers from the garden in summer—to the sick, the lonely, the bereaved. Going to someone's home was one thing, but the hospitals and funeral homes were scary at first. Other times might find us in an old cemetery weeding the graves of relatives I never knew and leaving a pickle jar of flowers. As I got older, I might be sent into someone's kitchen to do the dishes while my mother visited with people too sick or sad to see to it themselves. She became a 4-H leader and nurtured a crowd of neighborhood girls. When she retired, she volunteered at church and continued with 4-H. That's why applying to the Peace Corps seemed like a no brainer to me.

Months passed, and I received the letter that I got in and was being assigned to teach English in the Philippines. That would have really launched me into the world, but I had hit a speed bump. Much to my surprise, I had fallen in love, quite hopelessly, and didn't want to be a world away from the man I ended up marrying. I had never thought about being married, never had what girls in the fifties had—hope chests. Once, one of my friends proudly showed me hers. She lifted the cedar lid, and there were neat stacks of dishtowels. Why in the world would you hope for a life of washing dishes? It wasn't that I hated kids or marriage; it's just that it didn't seem to have anything to do with me. Then in my last semester at college, an old high school friend set me up with a blind date. This guy, according to her, was perfect for me. He had gone to Catholic school from kindergarten through college—I hated church. He had a motorcycle. I couldn't ride a bicycle. He had grown up in a foreign country and spoke another language. I was provincial as the potatoes in my mother's garden. He could fly a plane. I had never flown at all. All my dating to that point had been at an emotional arm's length. I went out to have a good time, and that was it. When I walked into her apartment, I saw my date. He was getting something out of the refrigerator, and I thought, "Oh, shit." I knew he was the one. With what seemed like absolutely nothing in common, he was it. Three months later, he figured it out too, and we married the following year. The Peace Corps adventure evaporated.

While Wally was still my boyfriend, he took me to the local airport, in the middle of acres of corn, for my first flight. The pilot of the two-seater plane opened the door and motioned me inside. The seat I was headed for was the pilot's because it was a five-dollar flying lesson. We buckled up and slammed the puny doors shut, and he started the engine. Then we proceeded down the runway, and he had me pull back on the yoke in front of me and do the takeoff. All I could see was the sky, the propeller, and the metal skin of the plane that looked to be slightly thicker than a fingernail secured with loose rivets and paste. It was 1965. I loved it.

My second flight, a few months later, was another story entirely. We took off from the same airfield, but I was in the back of a four-seat plane. It was a winter night, and it was cold and windy. The boyfriend was having the lesson this time. The wind was so bad we were tossed

9

like cookies at the end of a carnival ride. The instructor had warned us the conditions were bad, but we were hearty, we were game, we were nuts. Our landing was crablike, but the wheels finally grabbed the tarmac. I stopped praying not to die, and then the engines revved. Dear God, we were going to do touch-and-goes, numerous practice takeoffs and landings. I was soon so airsick I was praying, if not for death, at least a teensy crash landing to relieve my suffering. Please, God, just a broken leg, a few cuts and bruises; just get this plane on the ground and let me out. By the third landing, I had thrown up into my leather gloves and felt much better. That's when the prayers made another 180—please, Mary, Mother of God, save me. I don't want a broken leg. I didn't mean it, honest, Jesus. Can't you recognize a lie? Eventually, my scrambled prayers were answered, and I was beyond relieved when finally the plane did not rev but turned and taxied to the hangar. It had been so noisy in that plane and so airy neither the pilot nor the instructor knew I had been sick. I was, in fact, congratulated on being a great passenger under terrible conditions. I smiled, said nothing, and fled to the airport bathroom to toss those gloves. It was probably that night flying practice that prepared me for a dicey landing in the Himalayas decades later.

Useful Life Lessons for Travel

With only a few commercial flights here and there as needed, I spent the next twenty-one years living my life with my husband, Wally, settled in the country in the mountains of Virginia. I still thought about traveling, but opportunities weren't coming along. I seemed to think I needed reasons for travel. However, living in the country taught me something useful for when I eventually learned to take off. Early in our time there, Wally would spend summers doing marine research at Woods Hole on Cape Cod. My work as an editorial assistant at Virginia Tech didn't give me summers off, so we arranged to see each other every three weeks for a long weekend. It was my first night alone in the country that I realized I was not just scared; I was terrified. I would go to bed early—television reception practically didn't exist—and something would wake me. Heart thumping and eyes bugging out of my head, I would get up and look around. Nights were cool in the mountains, and we had no air conditioning, so the windows were open. I could have heard anything—deer, bear, or homicidal maniac, most certainly the last. Everyone was armed to the teeth out there. If you didn't have a gun rack in your pickup, you were taken for a visitor or some kind of liberal pussy. More than once, while getting ready for work, I would pass by the back door and realize that not only had I not locked it, I hadn't even closed the damned thing. It didn't help that one night some grizzled farmer friends, who had come over to help me with the cattle, asked me if I had a gun. They said they wouldn't live alone where I did without one. The gravity of the situation was emphasized by a stream of tobacco juice that just cleared my sneakers.

We had guns, but I had no interest in them and wasn't sure where they were or how to use them. At one point, I got a dog and kept her outside at night. Pretty soon, I had to find a nice home for her because she heard things at night and barked and woke me up, and both of us wanted to howl. Then one night, when I woke with terror in my veins, I realized that I just could not go on like that. I had to give up the fear like a habit that might kill me. I moved through the little house in the dark, peering out into the night through the window screens. The throbbing noise of summer insects seemed to push back, as though the night had a pulse. I realized, this was the way it was in this remote place and that I could accept it or continue to make myself crazy. If someone actually wanted to find me hidden away out there, break into my house, and kill me, well, that would be the way it ended. Then I would be dead, as I eventually would be anyhow. The rational side of me knew a break-in was statistically more likely to happen in a city than where I was. God help me, it worked. This turned out to serve me well on a midnight train to Warsaw on my first trip abroad.

Another skill that served me later was sailing. In spite of the fact that we were about as far away as we could get from an ocean in a state that bordered one, Wally decided he needed to learn to sail. There is a 20,600-acre manmade lake two hours from where we lived in Virginia, and that's where we began a long experience with sailing. Our first attempts were downright laughable and sometimes dangerous, but we survived our way through ownership of three sailboats, each progressively larger and faster. It was when we owned the 22-foot Catalina and started racing that I reached a moment of crisis. The crux of the problem, I decided, was that Wally was in control of the boat, and Wally was an idiot. Unfortunately, I couldn't prove it. The only way to rectify this was to learn to sail the boat myself. He willingly ran all the lines back to the cockpit so that one person could both steer and handle the sails. Eventually, I soloed, and we became partners (pretty much) instead of adversaries. It also boosted my confidence to be able to take our boat out and bring it back and dock it all on my own. Sailing alone presented situations that had to be solved if you wanted to get back to land. It was difficult for me to start the outboard engine on the Catalina, so I had to figure out how to get where I wanted to go entirely by sailing. It turned out to be good practice for my first trip abroad alone when there were no cell phones, I didn't know the language on the pay phone instructions, and I had to call the U.S. You figure out how to solve a brand new problem when you have to.

First Trip Alone

Finally, an opportunity came along that sent me on a trip alone and for my own reasons. It was twenty-two years after that first flight in the cornfield. I was 44, and, like so many in their forties, thought I had one foot on a banana peel and the other in the old folks' home. I decided I wanted to go to a writers' conference presented by the Island Institute in Sitka, Alaska. It was a small conference and stressed concerns about the environment. Wally's only prediction, when I asked what he thought, was that I would be the only woman there who shaved her legs. Off I went, smooth as silk.

The conference was held at a small college. We stayed in the dorms and ate fish, fresh off the local boats. We had sent our work ahead to have it read by the featured writers. Then we scheduled individual conferences with them as well as readings to the entire group. Discussing my poetry with Gary Snyder was such a privilege I was quite nervous. He had done his homework by reading the manuscripts we had sent ahead, and when we were introduced the first day, he referred to the deer in my poems as no doubt being a "whitetail" because I lived in Virginia, and that somehow set me at ease. It only continued to get better when, sitting around one evening, waiting for the nightly readings to begin, Gary, Nanao Sakaki, and a few of us entertained ourselves by demonstrating interesting noises a person could make with their bodies. Nanao, known for his poetry and his great ability to sit alone in the desert and meditate for long, serious times, could do a mean armpit fart. When Gary Paul Nabhan asked for a copy of one of my poems, I was amazed. All these accomplished writers were so kind.

Then, after a week away from Wally, I noticed how I tended to sit next to men wearing the kind of shirt he wore. Hmmm, good thing it was time to go home. The only way I could communicate with him was at a pay phone outside the dorm. No cell phones, no computers; no wonder I got lonely. The conference was great, but it was in Sitka, and Sitka rolled up its sidewalks anytime there wasn't a cruise ship in sight, and back then, that wasn't often. While an evening in a sailor's bar with pictures of what guys do on their boats at sea (get naked but for their hats and boots) was really interesting, I didn't need to go back every night.

It was June, so the sun only set for a few hours in the wee part of the morning, and people bopped 'til they dropped. It was easy to think you should go off for a walk in what seemed the shank of the evening only to discover it was closing in on midnight. Walks alone through the totem pole park, at any hour, were my first experiences of what I think of as my soul-souvenirs. There were no guides explaining the iconography of the treasures. The air was infused with the scent of pine, the path heavily mulched, and the place silent but for birds. Usually, no one else was around except for the puppy-sized slugs oozing across the trail here and there. As I leaned to examine these creatures, I didn't have a clue that, in the next decades, I would go on to get up close and personal with meerkats in the Kalahari Desert, moai on Easter Island, lonely Romanian babies, and so much more.

If I was becoming a traveler, it wasn't happening quickly, but what was holding me back? It wasn't my husband. I think it was the hidden but powerful force of "the way it's supposed to be." Although I was home all day with my father before I started school and my mother went to work every day, she also came home and cooked, cleaned, gardened, sewed, and helped on the farm. The message was clear: women had to do everything and then some. Maybe that's why it took so long for me to hit the road—I was standing in my own way. I was hanging onto some notion from the fifties that I couldn't go somewhere without my husband, a family member, or a friend. It would have been OK if I needed to travel for my work, but not on my own. The desire to go finally overcame the misconceptions, and my next adventure came nine years later. At age 53, I crossed the pond, and it was like the door to the planet opened. The key to that door turned out to be volunteerism.

Totem pole in Alaska along the Totem Pole path in Sitka, where the author discovered her first soul souvenir.

1

Poland,
Home for the First Time—
Age 53 (1996)

A Polish man greeted me at the Warsaw airport by bowing and kissing my hand. There may have been a bit of a click when his heels snapped together as well. Then he kissed my friend Kathy's hand. This man was certainly not the Polish version of a Walmart greeter. He was the director of the NOTORO Art Symposium come to welcome two of his American artists.

Kathy, my friend and fellow artist, and I had been juried into the symposium being held in Gdansk, Poland. We would be two of half a dozen Americans working at the Academy of Fine Arts in Gdansk. Kathy had been to Europe when she was in college. This trip was my first hop across the pond at the ripe old age of 53. It was time to get out into the world finally. The woman I had thought of as immortal, my mother, had died. Her death from cancer was fairly quick as she was diagnosed late into the disease. Because of that, it was a shock. She had a reputation as a wonderful woman, saintly but with a lot of fun about her. There is, in fact, a small street named for her near our old home. Since there is also a major highway there now, her name blazes from a huge green sign. Three years after her death, and much grieving, I was realizing it was time to emulate her adventurousness and take off. In addition, menopause had had its way with me. There's something about the biological sea change that arrives after crawling from the ovens fueled by hot flashes and night sweats that makes one realize this truly is the second half of life. Age 50 makes a statement, but freedom from the monthly cycles and all it implies hammers home the message with a sharp nail. The opportunity to travel (I still needed them) presented itself in this symposium. It seemed it was time to go, as I also could finally afford it, thanks to years of working and saving.

The director asked in English if we needed anything, and I mentioned a bathroom. He looked at me and hesitated, looked at the man with him (his driver), and then said, "There will be time to take a bath at my apartment before we leave for Gdansk." Now it was my turn to look confused and a bit embarrassed. Then I remembered one of my Polish aunts telling me the Polish word for toilet and rephrased my question. "Where is the *toaleta*?" I asked and looked around the terminal. Relief from comprehension spread through the group, and the WC was pointed out. Kathy and I headed towards the pointed direction, and the men followed. It was wise of Aunt Mary to come up with that word to teach me. I remember my grandparents on my mother's side speaking Polish, and my mother and her sisters remembered the language into adulthood—enough to switch into it when they didn't want me to know what they were talking about when I was a child.

We were soon off to his home, where we waited for his wife and two children to assemble, and some hours later, we all piled into a van and headed off on a five-hour drive north to Gdansk. While I was gazing out the window, my eyes begging for sleep, I watched enormous birds searching for grubs in the plowed fields, sauntering slowly on stilt legs. They were storks, my first European wildlife sighting, and it turned out to be a bird I had only related to fairy tales and folklore. There was a time in America when storks brought babies, bundled up in diaper slings hanging from their beaks. They were on all the baby shower invitations and birth announcements in the 1950s. The euphemism was, "She's expecting a visit from the stork." As we drove through a forested area, I saw people seated beside the highway and asked what they were doing—selling mushrooms they had collected. Suddenly I was back in the mountains of Pennsylvania where I grew up, and people, many of them Polish, sold wild huckleberries along the road. They had picked them where they grew rampant over the coalmines.

We arrived after dark, and somehow Kathy and I lost track of the rest of the party after checking into our room in the Angel House Pension. We stumbled out into the night and found our way to a restaurant, a menu in Polish, and a waiter who spoke no English. Hungry and tired, we pointed and hoped for the best. We lucked out: it was a chicken dish, and we enjoyed it. There was an odd drink on the menu, described as an American favorite, Red Bull. I had never heard of it. We did wish they used napkins, though. You have no idea how ingrained a napkin on the lap can be until it isn't there and you are left plucking at your pants.

All this was mesmerizing in its newness for me. The smallest things were a novelty—like the bedding. Each bed had a bottom sheet and a thick and heavy puffy cover on top encased in a cotton cover of its own—the duvet. Then there was a fluffy acrylic blanket with a rampant stallion on it—think velvet painting sort of art. When I lifted the duvet, it felt like it would crush me, so I slept on top and snuggled under my blanket and borrowed Kathy's as well. The night she demanded her blanket back, I learned to sleep under the duvet. If you worked it right, you could make a little tunnel under there that was warm and held up the half-ton of wadding.

Changing money was an adventure. Kathy and I decided to be terribly legal and go to the bank to get our złoty. We entered a typical marble-and-glass bank lobby and waited in line to find out what to do, then waited in another line to do it, then were passed off to another line and a person with a computer, then to a lady with a rubber stamp the size of a hatchet, which she wielded as though it were one. Finally, we got our cash and a bundle of documentation to go with it. We had no idea what all the paperwork was about. The next time we needed cash, we slipped into the cambio, pushed dollars under a glass window like we were buying movie tickets, then watched złoty riffle through a person's hands and come back under the window to us. Easy peasy, and off we went.

In 1996, Poland was still figuring out how to deal with free enterprise, and people were starting to purchase nice things for themselves. While there were new cars on the streets, most of them had anti-theft devices that seemed to go off, well, often. Some of these cars were personalized with outrageous fuzzy seat covers printed like cowhide, Dalmatian dogs, or just big dots. Gdansk was an in-country tourist destination, so we were in a great place to observe tourists, both foreign and domestic, with their gaudy car seat covers. Postcards for sale showed the rubble that was Warsaw in the Second World War. I

View from our hostel window in Gdańsk.

realized I didn't know if my country had been responsible for that dev-
astation. My father had been in the Army in World War II and served
in Europe, but I only knew the main facts I'd learned in school and forgotten and the funny stories he had told about his life in a supply job.
By discreetly asking my fellow Americans, I was relieved to discover

18

we had not demolished Warsaw. The Germans had bombed and taken that city in 1939. Learning history was compelling at the actual site.

Each morning we woke earlier than our breakfast was ready in the Angel House dining room, so Kathy and I would go to a little outdoor café on the waterfront for an espresso. It was there we watched middle-aged German ladies in well-cut suits and sensible walking shoes having beer for breakfast. Our own breakfast included fresh rye bread and butter, cold cuts and cheese, sliced vegetables and meat and eggs, plus a tepid glass of fruity water. We ate as though we were going to rake hay by hand, as we saw people doing in the countryside. After stuffing ourselves, we went to a small grocery and bought things for our lunch if we planned to work straight through the day. That's where I began to learn a few Polish words. The first, which sounded like something from an African language, was *woda niegazowana* (voda knee-ah-gaz-ah-wanna), which meant water without gas and referred to non-carbonated bottled water. After that came *tak* (tock) for "yes" and *nie* (nyeh)—Russian *nyet* without the "t" for "no." And of course, *hello, goodbye, please,* and *thank you*, which I proceeded to interchange at will.

Yogurt, fruit, bread and water in hand, we then walked to the academy and up the 74 steps to work in our shared studio. One day Kathy and I visited St. Mary's Church, the largest brick church in Europe, built in stages between 1350 and 1502. It's 346 feet long, 217 feet wide and can hold 25,000 people. We paid two złoty and climbed the bell tower, a spiral squeeze up 400 steps. Little did I know this would be the beginning of a travel habit, counting steps when there seemed to be a lot of them. Once at the top, enjoying the view of the shipyards, other churches and the city, we began to talk about this and that. We assumed the teenaged boy in the Chicago Bulls tee shirt (everyone had one) was Polish. Suddenly he startled us by asking, "Where're you from?" in American English. Can't tell the natives without a scorecard.

One Sunday, I decided to revisit my Catholic roots and went to Mass at St. Mary's. Like any massive place, it is difficult to convey the scale, but suffice it to say, when babies became restless mothers wheeled them around the side aisles in their prams, and it was not an interruption. They were way out there on the perimeter. This going-to-church routine would become a habit in my travels, sort of an homage to my mother, who dragged me there every Sunday and Holy Day—with hat, gloves and prayer book to keep her girl holy.

When we weren't working, we shopped and explored. That's how I discovered that I like to buy ordinary things for souvenirs, like dishtowels and socks. I loved the market—where we learned not to touch the merchandise but to point. There I bought a wooden kitchen tool, a sort of knob on a handle. We still use it to bang lids that don't want to unscrew. I have no clue what it is supposed to be used for. My favorite souvenir from that trip is a small wooden bird with wings and wheels. It's about the size of a man's fist, and the wings flap when the bird rolls. The whole thing was hand carved and assembled by an old man who sat in the square most days and whittled them. He made the wings and wheels work using found wire and decorated them with lines and dots using red and black ballpoint pens. I couldn't understand how much he wanted, so I held out a handful of coins, and he took the price. It has become one of my prized possessions, and I am a person who loves to toss stuff.

Every weekday, we went off to our studios. The painters each had a huge space, and Kathy and I shared another large one. Kathy is a paper artist and had brought the papers and paint and tools she would need. I had brought sheets of thin copper, aluminum foil, paint, sketchbook, etc. Gdansk did not have much in artists' materials at the time, and we were warned that painters might be using house paints. I had brought the foil because I had devised a way to make it look like gold by painting it with amber shellac.

When we weren't working, our hosts took us to interesting places—for instance, a building without power where poor university art students worked on their paintings. We were treated to a bonfire with beer and roasted sausages. There I met a dog that knew how to behave better than any I had ever met in the U.S. The bowl of sausages to be cooked was on a chair at just his nose height, and although he sniffed deeply, he never touched them. Instead, he and a cat sat by the fire, and if a sausage fell off a stick, they sprang up and, working together, gingerly pawed it out of the ashes and carefully ate it. Little did I know this would become a cultural indicator for me in future travels. How the dogs behave and how people behave towards them can tell you a lot about a culture and its economy.

The author in the studio at the Academy of Fine Arts in Gdańsk (courtesy Kathy Guest).

Another day, we visited Hitler's world headquarters, Wolf's Lair, a secret city of bunkers that he and several thousand Germans inhabited for nearly three years of the war. The place is in an area that used to be East Prussia, a part of Germany until 1945. It was an all-day excursion because first, we stopped at Holy Linden, a Basilica devoted

Kathy Guest in the studio at the Academy of Fine Arts in Gdańsk, working on her paper art.

to the Virgin Mary in Mazury, Poland. Now a baroque architectural testimony to what money devoted to faith can accomplish, it began as a 15th-century chapel to which pilgrims traveled to visit a Linden tree. The story goes that in the 13th century, a convict was saved by the Virgin Mary herself. She visited him in his cell the night before his execution and gave him wood and a knife and instructed him to carve something, and then to hang it in a tree. Talk about artistic incentive.... His work was so stunning the judge believed his story of the holy visitation. He was freed and hung the piece in a Linden tree on his way home, thereby proving once again what I have always believed: art can save a person. Miracles began to take place at the tree where he had hung the carving, and pilgrims flocked to the site. It's possible the same area had been revered in pre-Christian times. This was my first lesson in the longevity of spiritual matters, as I visited a place of worship still in use but built on what might have been early tribal sacred ground.

From this lovely place, we continued on to Wolf's Lair. While bouncing in the van through the countryside, our hosts told us of the retribution taken after a failed assassination attempt at the Lair. Not all Germans were happy with the way the war was going towards the end, and there was at least one plot hatched within German forces to eradicate their leader. On July 20, 1944, Colonel Claus von Stauffenberg delivered the explosives meant to kill Hitler and some of the top command at the field headquarters towards which we were barreling. As we all know, it did not work and left one supremely pissed-off Fuehrer. Not only were all those suspected of taking part in the plot rounded up, but their friends and families were as well—7,000 arrested and nearly 5,000 killed. Our host, Isa, turned in her seat, tilted her lovely face, and pointed a finger under her chin to explain how the murdered were hanged "like pigs" for all to see, great meat hooks through their jaws. The dignity and holiness of the basilica were slipping away with the miles as we neared the compound.

During the war, Wolf's Lair had an airstrip and railroad line, a power station, a casino, and a movie theater—all concealed with camouflage. When we visited, it turned out to be an eerily beautiful place overgrown with trees and vines, no sign of the paved streets. The bombed-out concrete and twisted steel building parts were hidden among the trees and undergrowth. Because the concrete bunker walls were two meters thick, the chunks were as huge as the kind of ruins one sees in jungles, parts of ancient civilizations, but for the rusted iron bars poking through the vines. Unlike at many historic sites, there was little visitor information. We paid to get into the area, but other than a model of the complex in a building and postcards of some kittens in smeary 3-D, I remember little else. Once there, we walked quietly down silent forest paths studying the past made strangely beautiful, but still seeming to emanate evil. Alone and deep in my thoughts, I was surprised to turn at a tree and confront a wrinkled old woman in long black dress, apron, and babushka, tilting her head and smiling her few teeth at me. She was holding up an elaborate lace tablecloth for me to buy, I assumed. It was such a surprise. I just smiled, said nothing, and continued down the path. Allied forces never found the site, and the Germans destroyed it themselves to keep it from the advancing Russian Red Army before retreating to Berlin at the end of the war. Could the old woman with the tablecloth have been a girl living nearby then? Could she have known any of the soldiers or covertly watched them come and go in the heavy cars of the time? It was the beginning of many changes in perspective that travel would hand me in unexpected ways.

Another time, we were taken out into the country to visit a local artist. There was a bonfire in the back yard, and again, it was so like my rural childhood home in Pennsylvania. Back then, no one minded if

At Wolf's Lair, a boy poses as though he is holding up the massive chunks of concrete left after the Germans destroyed Hitler's secret headquarters so the enemy wouldn't get it.

you started a fire on your own property to sit around and enjoy. Inside the house, there was a banquet laid out on a table in the living room/ art gallery. When I enquired about a dish I did not recognize, my hostess dipped into it with a butter knife and spread a generous amount onto a thick slice of homemade bread, then handed it to me and said, "lard." Of course, I ate it and quickly realized it was pan drippings that had cooled to a spreadable consistency.

Outside the charming, restored section of Gdansk, with its cobblestones, stone buildings and town hall, there were plenty of huge concrete apartment buildings that our hosts apologetically dismissed as "communist architecture." Although the buildings were devoid of style, the residents livened them up with window boxes of flowers on the balconies and potted plants in the hallways—clay pots of begonias and ferns, as well as tomatoes. We visited some people living in one of these "blocks" and discovered double-door systems at each apartment. Going home meant unlocking a robust steel door and then unlocking another exactly like it and smack up against it.

Just as the American Civil War is still lingering in the U.S., World War II was still fresh in Poland in 1996. We learned that

Far right graffiti, perhaps left by skinheads.

visiting Germans spoke English to get better service—the Poles hated them. There was swastika graffiti painted on walls and skinheads' crimes reported in the newspapers.

One of our tour guides was an old man with the kind of accent you hear in movies about World War II. We met him for a tour in the lobby of Angel House. He was wearing a suit, tie, overcoat to his ankles, and baseball cap. He seemed to be about my father's age. When he mentioned people being sent to the camps, he said, "Kemps," and I wondered if he might have had to go there or had lost family there. When I read about workers finding a 1,100-pound World War II bomb in Warsaw years later in 2012, I wondered what the oldest people in the population thought about it and what the teenagers thought about it. When does that shadow become slight enough to ignore? Must it loom until a larger shadow overtakes it?

It was easy to go off on my own in Gdansk. And that is when I was mistaken for a Pole. I am half Polish, and people would come up and speak to me, at some length, in Polish. I had to inform them, gently in English, that I didn't understand. Then they would quickly flee, whether from embarrassment or because they had just tried to engage me in an illegal transaction; I don't know. There was one young man who dropped some money as he whizzed by on rollerblades. I shouted, and he stopped and saw me waving the money at him. He came back, took it with a smile, and began talking to me. We leaned companionably against a railing looking out at the ships in the harbor, and he went on, and I chuckled and nodded where I thought appropriate. Then he smiled, waved, and skated away. It seemed like a very nice conversation, or maybe I had agreed to meet him at midnight for a drug deal. Between the language business and watching an old woman bend from the waist, knees straight, to clean a stoop, just the way my mother, grandmother, and aunts all did—and some of the foods we ate—I felt I had tapped into the scraps of Polish life my grandmother and great grandmother had unknowingly left me. It reminded me of a line by Gabriel Garcia Marquez in his novel *Of Love and Other Demons*, when his character found himself in a foreign place and was surprised that he "recognized his hereditary nostalgia."

I learned on that trip that I am not fussy about foreign food. After all, the lard was great. Looking for lunch one day, Kathy and I spotted

Top: View of the harbor a half-block from our hostel. *Bottom:* The *Szafir* (sapphire) docked near the center of old town Gdańsk.

27

people eating what looked like hot dogs. We followed the line until we found the source under a set of stairs leading to a government building in the square. A woman took your money and handed it down then, in a while, a hand came up out of the gloom holding a hot dog dressed with lettuce and tomatoes, quite tasty. I also discovered that my mother's pierogi recipe was actually Russian style—and that the fruit water we had at breakfast was made by boiling a small amount of fruit and then serving the liquid as a juice. My oldest Polish aunt remembered it from her childhood in the mountains with the coalmines and berry picking.

Because I sometimes used found objects in my artwork, I was always looking for things on the street. Well, truth be told, I had been picking stuff up off the road since I was six and started walking to school. Broken glass was a favorite back then. My mother would find blue, clear, green, and of course, beer-bottle-brown bits of glass in the pockets of my dresses. She said I was like a crow and was attracted to anything shiny. However, this turned out to be a problem in Gdansk because everything was clean as a whistle. Every morning people were sweeping the streets and washing cobblestones with a bucket and rag. Entrepreneurs picked up old cardboard for recycling. There were no idle newspapers to be had. The best I could do was a broken piece of porcelain tile, a pigeon feather, and a German penny. Then one day, I just spread my sketchbook on the cobblestones in front of the Art Academy and made a rubbing with a pencil. That turned into a copper wall piece titled *Cobblestones of Gdansk*, years after I had returned home and is now in someone's art collection in Virginia.

Sometimes we would see a child, well dressed and clean, kneeling on the street, head bowed, holding a small hand-lettered cardboard sign. I asked one of our hosts about it, and she simply said it was gypsies and kept going. I never found out if they were begging or quietly making a political statement.

To communicate with Wally, I had to go to the Post Office during the day and buy a phone card from a *pani* (more about them later). Then I had to go to a payphone on the street in the square at night because of the time difference. We were able to get faxes at the academy, so he sent me one, but it took days for anyone to find me and deliver it. At least we weren't sending letters on clipper ships back and forth.

I would stand in the dark, windy square, phone in hand, watching the bar that measured the time I had left to hear Wally's voice dwindle, and speak or listen until the last "I love you."

After two weeks, it was time to leave, and our hosts arranged for Kathy and me to take a late train to Warsaw to catch our plane the next morning. The day before, Isa took Kathy and me to the train station to make the arrangements. Kathy and I had observed what we referred to as power *pani*. *Pani* means lady or woman in Polish, and initial formal conversations usually begin with the term *prosze, pani* (pro-sha pawnee), sort of, "Excuse me, madam," and then the request would be made. Power *pani* seemed to be everywhere in some official capacity. At an art opening, they were on duty in their suits and no-nonsense shoes, one in each room; their main duty seemed to be glowering, and they were excellent at it. When a glass framed sign fell off a wall at the art show, the sociable noise that is an opening stopped completely. The power pani approached, looked down at the broken glass, and spread a few of the shards with the toe of her shoe. It was as though we were all holding our breath. Then she clasped her hands behind her and walked slowly away, sturdy heels clicking like some kind of moral accounting machine. We all heaved a sigh and went back to our wine glasses and chatter. Apparently, no one would be jailed for this offense.

Kathy and I had also noticed that Poles often seemed to shout at each other during normal conversation. Not when they were telling me things on the street—that was all confidential and quiet. At the train station, we got to see an interaction with a power *pani* up front and personal. It began when Isa politely, and in a normal voice, said to the *pani* behind the window, "Prosze, pani," and the *pani*, expressionless as a brick, nodded politely. Then Isa began shouting in Polish about these two *pani* (Kathy and me) needing one-way, first-class tickets to Warsaw on the midnight train, (and from here I invent) right now, this minute, and I want no nonsense from you, you minor railroad official. Power pani takes a breath and screams back that there aren't any first-class tickets left, so just get off your high horse and tell the foreign bitches they can travel like the rest of us mere mortals. Isa screams some more (no doubt about the bitch part). Back and forth. Finally, two third-class tickets are produced, money is exchanged, and Isa tells the *pani* "thank you" in a polite and pretty voice. Poker face nods agreeably and waits for her next transaction.

At the train station, near midnight, we were kissed in the sweet Polish way—three times; one cheek, the other, then back to the first. We were taken to a compartment with three, maybe four bunks on each side, a Polish family already ensconced and mostly tucked in, lights out. We had the top bunks—as we arrived last. A young man in the group heroically lifted my bag all the way to my bunk, but just couldn't heave Kathy's up for her. I climbed the ladder and lay down in the narrow space. Kathy asked how in the world we would know when to get off the train. I said I had no clue, thought about how I would be so dead if the train went upside down in a river, closed my eyes, and eventually slept, the ceiling only inches from my face. What I had learned those scary nights alone in the Virginia countryside still worked. Assess the situation, and if no action can be taken, close your eyes and go to sleep. Sometime in the night, the old man in the bunk below woke with a nightmare, shouting in Polish, and sending up clouds of garlic breath. Then we all settled down again until we thought maybe it was time to get up. Out we went into the teensy hallway with our bags. I was practicing out loud how to say, "Where is the airport?" in Polish when a voice in American English said, "Just follow us." Thank God.

The train came into the underground Warsaw station, and we successfully got off, two nervous nellies, Kathy dragging her herniating bag up and down the stairs. The people we were supposed to follow had disappeared. No one seemed to be around except young men dressed in black sniper outfits, patrolling with what looked like automatic weapons. I went up to one of them and asked my rehearsed question, never thinking that I wouldn't understand a word of his answer. He helpfully began a long stream of Polish, and best of all, he pointed. That is when I learned to get around anywhere in the world. Learn enough of the language to ask, and they will point. Follow the point until you need to ask again, or you arrive at your destination.

On that trip, I had the first experience that only happens to me when I travel. There comes a moment when it's as though I can feel myself standing on the slowly moving earth, existing where I have never been before. I am aware of how far I am from the place I live and from the people I love, my base camp. It is both a personal and global perspective. The first time was standing on the cobblestones in Gdansk at night, the wind blowing what little bit of grit there was to blow. I had just used a phone card at a street phone to call Wally. The time had run out on the card, the little light on the display had gone out, and I hung up the phone and stood in the dark. Although it was night, the sky was fading between turquoise and purple, and a planet was clearly visible above the clock tower in the square. It was a feeling of being alone on the planet yet perfectly at one with it. I realized it was a soul souvenir.

2

Poland,
Crossing the Pond Alone—
Age 57 (2000)

I wanted to travel more, but something was holding me back. I had read issues of *Ms.*, the pioneering feminist magazine started by Gloria Steinem in 1971; *The Feminine Mystique*, published in 1963 and written by Betty Friedan; and *Our Bodies, Ourselves*, now in 30 languages. It's difficult for today's young women to understand the time when I was growing up. *Ms. Magazine* was the first to address the political ramifications of the educated American women's situation. They published researched articles on subjects like pay discrepancies and quotas on women at universities. Educated women of presumed privilege began to take a closer look at their lives and acknowledge their dissatisfaction. During World War II, women went to work in factories. That's where my mother got her start. When the war ended and the men came home, the women discovered they were expected to give the jobs back to the men and go keep house and raise children. My mother didn't do that. She kept working. Without an education, she did not expect to have a job that paid more than the one she had, but she worked hard and seemed to like it. She worked for more than 40 years and only retired because they closed the plant. Women who had earned one or two degrees were also expected to stay home raising children, keeping house and entertaining. These were the women who were questioning their identities.

I was teaching high school English when those publications hit the streets, and I, too, looked. I found out men at the school where I was employed, with the same education and years of experience I had, were paid more. The reasoning was they had families to support or had been in the military. Women were matter-of-factly considered supplementary earners. *The Feminine Mystique* laid out "the problem that has no name." Too many of us had accepted the notion that we were just sexual beings/cleaners and cooks. When I went to college, the jokes were: women wanted a degree, all right, a Mrs.—and a good marital match was concerned with incompatibility: his income and her "patability." *Our Bodies, Ourselves* was cheaply printed, and we were all wearing the ink off the newsprint pages as we passed it around to find out what our bodies really were all about. A predominance of male doctors had been patting us on the heads for generations and telling us everything was fine—women just didn't have heart attacks, for example. It certainly surprised one of my aunts when one killed her. It's true that I passed on the opportunity to join a group of women readers of *Our Bodies…* armed with plastic speculums, flashlights, and plenty of wine to have a look-see at each other's reproductive interiors. I considered myself liberated anyhow, annoyed with the slow progress, but liberated. Still, there was that nagging low-grade infection of a thought that to travel alone was not the way it was supposed to be. It was reinforced every time someone asked me something like:

"You went to Alaska alone? Weren't you scared?"
(Should I have been? What was wrong with me that I wasn't scared?)
"Did you cook meals ahead and freeze them for your husband?"
(Did people actually do that?)
Or my favorite, "What did your husband do while you were gone?"
(How could I possibly know this?)

Finally, at long last, it dawned on me that if I was going to see the world, I had to stop waiting around for someone to take me or come along with me, or to somehow gain permission. I realized that needing opportunities was holding me back. I needed to pack my bag and go. I also felt financially secure enough and had totally rid myself of the confusion so many of my generation drag around with them about "our money." Too often, I've experienced this as meaning that the husband's reasons for spending are always good and the wife's reasons for spending are questionable at best. The reality, in our marriage, is that I can spend it, and he can spend it, and neither of us is out to break the bank. Women may read books on liberation, but many of us still confuse our roles as obedient daughters with partner/wives. I had been standing in my own way, and it was time to step aside.

Four years after the trip with Kathy, I was ready to do it. I started thinking about the nuts and bolts of a trip—what would be the best way? A tour did not appeal to me, maybe because the first trip wasn't one. Then, with an interest in returning to Poland, I came across a tiny newspaper announcement about a local man who had gone to Poland on a volunteer vacation with Global Volunteers, a nonsectarian organization offering volunteer vacations around the world. I called him up and asked him about it. I got Global's catalog, applied, was accepted, and bought a round trip ticket to Warsaw. My thinking was that I would be taken care of. My meals were provided, I had a place to stay, and I would be in one place the entire time getting to know local people through the work I would be doing. And, it was tax-deductible. Yes, you pay to do volunteer work. With Global Volunteers, I was teaching English again. No experience was needed, except the ability to speak English, of course. We would be trained, provided with materials, and helped along the way.

The night before my trip, the airline called and said they had to reschedule my flight, and I would arrive in Warsaw later than expected. Without thinking for a second that I had to accept this, I said that wouldn't do. They said, "OK." And that was that.

Wally took me to the airport, kiss-kiss, and I was off to a hub where I finally looked at my boarding pass. I was traveling business class across the Atlantic to Germany. It was lovely, and it spoiled me tremendously. Wine presented in a bottle, label ready for inspection as though, if you didn't want that one, they could tromp on down to the wine cellar and fetch another. Real food on real plates and a seat I could actually sleep in—ahhhh. However, once in Germany, well, that's when it hit the fan. I had a long layover, and when it was time to go to the Polish airline for the last leg, they refused to let me get on the plane— some glitch somewhere. I was even ready to buy another ticket—no dice. The power *pani* in charge wasn't giving an inch, even though I had a little power *pani* in me, thanks to my Polish mother. However, the bottom line, being half a *pani* just wasn't enough to get me past the real thing.

I went back to the first airline and made a plea for help. There was much keyboard pounding and a few "shits" from the woman trying to solve my problem. Yes, Germans think nothing of using that word casually. Finally, I got a ticket to Amsterdam and another one to Warsaw. I would arrive at midnight instead of noon. The plan was to be met at the airport and then driven, for about an hour, to the town where I would be staying. Because I wasn't going to be on the flight they planned to meet, I needed to call a number in the U.S. and leave a message so that they could call the people in Poland about the change in arrival time. With some luck, I would be picked up when I actually arrived, and they wouldn't travel to the airport more than necessary. That was before everyone and his Chihuahua had cell phones. The directions on how to use the payphones (remember them?) were in German. I speak English and a smattering of French, and that's it. Somehow, I figured out how to call the U.S. and leave the message. Then, while I was at it, I called Wally and told him what had happened.

As I neared the last leg of the trip, I began to wonder what I would do if the volunteer people weren't there to pick me up at midnight. My destination was too far to take a cab, and besides, I didn't have the actual address. So I looked around the Amsterdam waiting area at the others on my flight and tried to figure out who might speak English and who might help me. I settled on a young Polish woman who was in a zone of her own, just coming back from China. I asked her if I needed to spend the night, would she recommend a hotel. Pretty soon, she offered to take me to her apartment. I assured her that would not be necessary; a hotel recommendation would be fine. It was a little like sailing alone, what would I do if the wind came up—think ahead.

Finally, we got to Warsaw, and the luggage carousel went 'round and 'round and did not bring my bag. Used to taking matters into my own hands by now, I looked around and spotted it behind a counter and an official-looking rope. Sleep-deprived and still working on my inner power *pani*, I simply went around the rope and got it. A nice young Polish woman in high heels and short skirt clip-clopped her way to me and told me in English. "Ah, your luggage has descended before you." I couldn't argue with that; it had indeed because it was put on the plane I should have been on, #@*%&^, I thought. Now I just needed to go through "control," she informed me, nicely rolling the "r" to lengthen the word, and I would find out if my ride was there.

It was. I profusely thanked the young Polish woman I had met in Amsterdam and set off with the American Global Volunteer team leader and the Polish driver for Reymontówka, a 19th-century manor house converted to a conference center.

I was shown to my room, blessedly free of a roommate because we were an uneven number. The room was old and elegant with ceilings so high I thought clouds might form up there. There were nice draperies, two single beds—one for me and one for my junk—a desk, reading lamps, and a spigot sticking out of the wall at the head of one of the beds. Seemed handy, but I didn't know for what. Best, it had an adjoining toilet and sink with a shared shower down the hall. It didn't take me long to lift that heavy Polish slab of a duvet and get down to sleeping.

The next morning, having slept through my alarm, I was awakened by a banging on my door and told breakfast was ready. Our family-style meals were hearty fare, and I loved it all. Having gone through menopause, I was getting into a fattening-up phase that I would later need to beat with a stick. In the meantime, I heaped my plate with whatever was offered and then got in line at the end of the meal to scrape the few leavings into a container taken to feed the pigs on the farm next door, whom we visited one day in all their porky splendor. One evening, we dined in an elegant room in the manor with a fire in the fireplace and vodka toasts all around. We learned the Polish toast, *na zdrowia*, which sounds a little like "next door d'ya," in a Jersey accent.

Fortunately for me, we had a day of instruction on how to teach and how to behave so that we would be good guests in this country. Otherwise, I might have been snoozing in the classroom from jet lag. The next day we visited the schools. I hadn't been a teacher in 25 years, and then I was teaching high school students. These younger kids were going to be a new experience. We went to different schools at different times of the day and spent our off hours preparing lessons. I quickly started a little domestic routine by washing my shirts and undies in my own sink and, after they stopped dripping, hanging them on a hanger from my chandelier to dry while I was gone all day.

In the morning, I was at a private Catholic school with small classes and a lot of attention to detail—like collecting the students to watch a real piece of biology as the school's pet snake slowly devoured its mouse lunch. One morning there the young priest who spoke English was telling me about the wonderful time he had meeting Pope John when he visited Poland. In the middle of it, one of my charming little girls yanked on his pant leg and told him something in Polish that made him and everyone else laugh. He had recently had his hair cut, and she wanted him to know he looked like an owl. At least they didn't take themselves too seriously. If I had said that to the priest at my church when I was little, the floor would have opened, and I would have been shooting straight to hell, express.

The kids I taught in the afternoon were at a large public school, and they were a handful. Their ages were around 10 or 11, and we met after school in May. The weather was glorious, and I would have rather been outside, so I'm sure they wanted to be there. We would arrive at the school while it was still in session. It was so different from American schools. When the bell rang and they poured out of the classrooms, it was bedlam, and no one seemed to care. Kids cheerfully flung each other down the stairs, whooping and laughing all the while. One afternoon, to the delight of my students, I followed one of my renegade boys into the boys' restroom and pulled him by the pants back from the window he was climbing out of—on the second floor. He was the same kid who taught me how to split a fresh maple tree seed and stick it to my nose. One day one of the boys didn't show up, and I asked, "Where's Luke?" There were many puzzled looks, but it was clear one boy knew the answer. He ran up to the Polish/English dictionary I had and thumbed through it, then wrote on the blackboard, "Luke escape." That was one way of putting it. On the last day, these little hellions came to class with bouquets of flowers and boxes of chocolates for me. It was all I could do to get them to share the candy with me—so polite. And it was very good chocolate.

When we weren't preparing our lessons or teaching, we had other opportunities, like visiting the orphanage down the road. The little girls seemed particularly hungry for some female attention, and I was cuddled on a couch by a small mob of them, one of whom gave me a little, but startling, love bite. Then I was pulled and pushed into one of their bedrooms and, with a lot of smiling and a secret sort of whispering, shown a beautiful child's long white dress. One of them would be soon taking her first communion, and it was all about the dress and the veil. I remember it well from when I donned my little white Mary

My public-school students working away like angels because there is a photographer in the room (courtesy Global Volunteers).

Janes, socks, and bridey outfit, folded my hands like an angel, and shyly advanced to where that scary priest was waiting to place a very dry piece of holiness on my tongue. I remember the dress, the veil, and the way the host stuck to the roof of my mouth. And believe me, those little Polish girls were right. It's all about the outfit.

Following the precedent I had established on my first trip abroad, I decided I would go to Mass on Sunday. Our in-country leader warned us of two things before we set out for the church. When foreigners attended, the priest liked to boost it up a notch, and we might find ourselves involved in more ceremony than usual. The other advice was that unlike in the U.S., where people wait in line and get into fights or at least glaring matches if someone cuts in front, Europeans do the opposite. If there is a space in front of you on the way to communion and you don't move ahead, expect Poles to slip right in there. And they did.

Having grown up with a Polish Catholic tradition, I was eager to see this church. When I would present myself dressed up for some event, and my mother thought I had gone a pair of earrings too far, she would say I looked like a Polish church at Christmas. Well, this one didn't seem overdone to me. And what was great was that it had dead ringers for my grandmother with their doughy shapes, fists full of rosary beads, tired-looking feet, and babushkas. The plaster saints were in their proper places, Mary on the left, Joseph on the right. Mary was particularly interesting as she had a portable electric heater stashed near her feet. No pretensions here, either.

As predicted, the priest paused and said a lot in Polish near the end. Then the altar servers (a young girl and boy) started hauling out holy paraphernalia that turned out to be a fancy parasol on a long pole, some meter-long sticks with cymbals, and an incense censor. Someone carried the parasol positioned over the priest's head as he swung the smoking censor, the kids banged the noisy sticks, and we all trooped out and took a turn around the outside of the church. Religion AND a show.

On the weekends, we were able to purchase tours and go away. For some reason, I thought about not going. One of our team members was a woman over 80. She asked if I was going. I said I might stay behind and rest. She said, "Oh, it doesn't take long to rest." I went. I saw Kracόw and toured Wieliczka, a salt mine that has been in operation since the Middle Ages. Even the Nazis used it. They built missiles inside it. There was a lake down there and a cathedral with chandeliers—all carved in salt. The elevator that took us into the section of the mine we toured held about four people, all touching each other. We were warned we would be in complete darkness during the descent. Not a ride for the claustrophobic.

Some of us went to Auschwitz and Birkenau. These were sobering places with tour guides who are formal and respectful. First, I noticed the famous sign at the entrance that reads "Arbeit Macht Frei" (Work Sets You Free). It was much smaller than I had in mind from photos and movies. This sign was to indicate to those arriving in the boxcars that they were there to work, not to die. The railroad tracks that brought the victims were there as though another train might come through at any moment. The second impression was surprise at how nice the little streets were in the area we toured first. This part had been a military barracks of red brick buildings, and the trees formed a pleasant walking area. Then we entered the buildings and were shown spaces so small a single person had to stand all night once forced to get inside.

The museum area contained large, plain rooms of wide board floors and display cases, one filled with shoes, another with hair, all of it grey or white, others with eyeglasses. Each case was the size of a small truck bed. No one smiled in this place. No one lapsed into idle chatter.

Birkenau required a short ride down the road to see the vast area that then just held outlines of the barracks that had been built for the tens of thousands of people housed there. Our guide showed us aerial photos, taken during the war, of the camp and its rail lines. One of our group asked if they were American images, and she said they were. We all filed back to our bus, quiet with thoughts of the horror of what we had seen represented and what could or could not have been done to end it sooner. I don't recall any discussion on our way back to the city. The pall of that place would not be dispelled. It was as though the very grass growing in the rail beds, 56 or more seasons of grass since the war ended, was still witness to the mountains of death created there.

We saw castles and palaces and learned the difference. The first is for defense—think heavy walls and small entrances; the second is a showy party place—Versailles, for example. But these are things you can see on television and read about in travel books.

My events are different. Like hearing a tinkling sound and turning to see an old woman in a dress and cotton headscarf walking with a teenaged boy down a paved road following a cow that was dragging the tinkling chain. I knew exactly what they were up to: taking the cow home to be milked at the end of the day. The cow knew the way and wanted to be milked, so she was in the lead. They had merely pulled up the metal stake to which her chain had secured her while she grazed all day. We had one milk cow when I was little, and as soon as I could heft the small sledgehammer, I was sent out to do the same thing. It works great for families with just one or two cows and no fences, and I had totally forgotten about it. I was back in Poland and yet also home again.

Then there was the realization that Poland has a deep love affair with their very own Chopin. While at Reymontówka, we were able to enjoy a piano competition. It was lovely to sit on the lawn and listen to the young pianists play as if they had been pressing the keys since birth. After the music, there would be applause, bouquets of flowers, kissing and bowing, accolades. And, of course, Chopin was featured by the most accomplished pianists. But the real inkling came when we were sightseeing on the weekends. Guides told us in hushed tones that Chopin's heart was entombed in this church, below this crypt, behind that bell tower. I was beginning to think they had minced it to get mileage out of such a relic.

There was also the driver who took us to the afternoon school—and developed a crush on me. One day, when I was still inside the school, he pantomimed to my fellow passenger, Dave, asking him if the two of us were married. Dave got it across emphatically that we were not. Then I heard from the staff that every year the man volunteered to drive and every year he got his heart broken. He had a very nice wife; I met her at the final party. It was all very interesting to me because, heading for 60, I was surprised anyone was looking at me other than Wally.

On that trip, I learned always to lock my door at night, no matter how safe I was. In addition to being out in the country and fenced in, a guard dog named Yogi (but spelled way differently) patrolled at night, and the place was secure enough for a politician. However, a group of visiting wood carvers was there with us one week, and one night one of them had had too much vodka. This caused him to forget where his room happened to be, so he did the only thing he could: he went up and down the halls, banging on and flinging open doors to find his bed. Talk about levitating from a sound sleep, can you imagine? I was glad I was down a side hall and that he didn't find my door.

That trip taught me a few things. One was: three weeks was too long away from home. I made nightly calls to Wally from a payphone in the lobby. It was easier than the phone card business on the previous trip, but without privacy. I also learned that when you go off alone, you don't need to look like yourself. If no one knows you, and the odds are astronomically against your running into someone you know, then you can do things differently. If you wear makeup, maybe you leave that at home or vice versa. Instead of bringing a hair dryer, I decided to put my wet hair up in pin curls—something I hadn't done since I was a kid. By morning it was dry, and it looked curly, and by noon it was straight as a poker again. But I didn't care; they didn't know what I usually looked like when equipped with hair products and implements. I'm not advocating looking bad, just different.

Somewhere I had heard about leaving things behind when you

One week, visiting wood carvers made these beehives. There is a tiny, bee-sized hole in each one for bees to enter (courtesy Global Volunteers).

go home, thus giving you more space in the suitcase for souvenirs. I had brought cheap shower shoes for this purpose, and I had some older shirts that were decent but didn't need to go back with me. The easiest was a full roll of toilet paper. I kept a wad in my purse should I need it on the road, blew my nose with it, and used the space it had taken up for a nice little replica of the Black Madonna of Częstochowa.

Most importantly, I learned that a volunteer vacation was a good way to travel alone. People who go on these trips are usually inveterate travelers and are willing to work. That mix makes for interesting people. They tend to be adventurous, diplomatic, and not too in love with themselves. That said, there was one volunteer who occasionally flew off the handle with one of us. Once it was with me. He was not an American. I had innocently asked another volunteer, who had traveled to Germany a great deal, if he had ever seen horse-drawn carts, like one we were just then passing, in Germany. He said he had not. That's when the other volunteer jumped all over me. He thought it absurd to ask such a question about an advanced country like Germany and pointed out that I was from the most powerful country on earth. I wasn't sure what that had to do with asking about a horse-drawn cart, but I was, of course, taken aback by the anger. I realized that, one, I didn't go around thinking about my country's status, and, two, what about all the Amish horse-drawn carriages and wagons I saw back home? I said nothing.

Travel was teaching me far more than I thought I'd learn. I was gaining perspective about my own country and myself as a representative—a representative of a very young country with a great deal of power dangerously linked with a limited experience of the toll of war. The railroad tracks at Auschwitz and the American aerial maps of the area haunted me.

3

Poland,
the Funniest Robbery
I Ever Experienced—
Age 59 (2002)

Two years passed, and I booked my first trip since 9/11. Some people talked of never flying again. I thought more statistically. It seemed to me that flying would be safer closer to the event than far from it; that is, the odds that such an extreme event would happen so quickly after the first seemed long. I headed back to Europe. Poland made me feel at home, so I signed up with another Global Volunteer project there. This one was in Zakopane, in the southern tip of the country—an area from which I suspected my grandfather had come. This idea was based solely on the tradition of wood carving in the area and evidence of his skill in that craft.

Zakopane is at the foot of the Tatra Mountains, and we were there in summer, staying at one of the many chalets that are filled with vacationing skiers in winter. We would be working with teenaged kids in a sort of summer language camp. Pam, the leader of the project, had called each of us and, based on our conversation, matched me with a great roommate, Marilyn. Our room was on the second floor. It had a slanted ceiling, purple shag carpeting, and a view from the window of the pine-covered mountains. The first night I slept with my head under the open window, and it rained a torrent. The duvet was thick and warm, and the cool, moist air delivered a peaceful sense of well-being. My sleep was deep because I was completely trusting, and that would have its consequences on this trip.

3. Poland, the Funniest Robbery I Ever Experienced

Marilyn and I worked with a small group of teenaged girls, young women, really, just outside our room in an open area near the stairs. It was pleasant to have students old enough, and in such small groups, that a noisy setting was not a problem. We were there to help them build their English language skills. Every afternoon we went off with the students on some kind of excursion. We strolled and mingled and learned from each other. It was at night that the students turned into real teenagers. They were in rooms one floor below ours, and music would pump out of there until all hours. One night, Marilyn couldn't stand it. She stormed downstairs in her pajamas and banged on the door until they answered. She told them to turn the music down. They agreed. She came back upstairs, crawled into bed, and was hit in the butt with the reverb from the bass line below. Down she goes—bang, bang, bang. Turn it down. Agreed. Close the door. This time she waited outside their door. When they turned it back up, she banged again and this time threatened I don't know what, but got her way. In the meantime, I knew nothing and was sleeping soundly—partly because of a developing hearing loss.

This trip had me being taken for a Pole again. One day I had wandered around town alone and was heading back before the others. I went to where the local bus waited and got onboard. Soon, a Polish woman seated across the aisle leaned over confidentially and told me all manner of things in that wonderfully sibilant language. As soon as I could, I revealed my illiteracy in her language, and she, as others had in Gdansk, quickly turned away and seemed very embarrassed as she crossed her legs, folded herself into her arms, and turned from me to look out her window. For me, these confusions were dear. My Polish family history was destroyed in the war, and there is probably no way to discover my roots in that country, much as I would like to do so.

As a child, sometimes my mother would stop my weeding lessons, and we would jump into the pickup truck and rush up the mountain to visit her grandmother. On the way, she taught me to say, "How do you do, Grandma?" in Polish. Great Grandma wore long cotton dresses with an equally long apron, cotton stockings and heavy shoes. Her face was creased from weather, and she was smiling, her hair pinned up in a wispy knot. She would come through her sapling gate carrying a stick and tapping her unruly dogs, which preceded her, barking and sniffing us onto the farm. I would sit quietly in her dim, cool house—with its metal bucket of well water and dipper resting on a small oilcloth-covered table—and listen to the two women talking in that shushing language. The house was small, and I could see both her large iron bed and the wood-burning stove she cooked on. She kept a rosary nested in a hollow of her pillow. The linoleum on the floor was spotless. I was content just to look around while they talked. Always there was one part that would make them both laugh until Great Grandma was wheezing and wiping tears. When it was time to light the coal-oil lamps, we would say goodbye. Then Mom would tell me the funny story on the way home, down the mountain, windows open for the cool evening breeze, lightning bugs blinking over moist summer fields. Is it any wonder being taken for a Pole meant so much to me? I didn't know I missed the sound of that language until I heard it again. I'm sure this feeling inspires those who work so hard to save dying languages—Godspeed to them.

One day we traveled south into Slovakia and toured the remains of an old castle, then visited a town with charming stone architecture. Alcohol was cheaper in Slovakia than in Poland, and Poles were lugging bags of bottles across the border in a steady stream. We saw a string of children at the castle on a school outing and realized they were Roma, most of them beautifully dark-eyed and dark-haired. I hadn't seen many since Gdansk. Some of us sat at a sidewalk café and enjoyed our coffee, then shopped a small grocery store where I bought dry soup mix and cat treats in packets with strange writing—and came away with souvenir Slovakian crowns in change.

In our travels, we saw interesting cemeteries. As a child, my mother would take me to family plots behind old churches where we would pull weeds, and I would learn about the people below—my great grandfather and his baby, who both died from influenza at the beginning of the 20th century, for instance. We often dug a little hole near the headstone, inserted an old jar of water and left fresh flowers in it. In Poland, graves were like friendly little backyards for the deceased. There were fences around them, plenty of plants, and occasionally, people sipping vodka and pouring one for the deceased onto the ground. In the evening, lighted candles in glass containers winked like tethered fireflies in the gathering darkness.

The complete trust I mentioned from the first night had been nurtured by my last trip to Poland. While we had been offered the use of a safe for our valuables at Reymontówka, the country manor turned into a conference center where we stayed, we had also been told that there had never been a robbery. Oh, one person had gone home missing a

Cemetery bench for visitors who come to commune with the departed.

camera once, but the following spring, it was found when the snow finally melted off the woodpile. That's why the most remarkable part of this trip turned out to be a robbery.

I was visiting with Pam in her room one day, and one of the volunteers came in looking worried. She announced that she had been robbed—from her room. I quickly took my leave so they could speak privately and went back to my room. Marilyn was there, and I told her what had happened. I then decided to check my suitcase, where I had stashed my extra cash. It was soft-sided, and I had attached a lock to the zipper—how ridiculous is that? Said lock was intact, but the thing opened right up as the thieves had somehow disabled the zipper without appearing to harm it at all. Sure enough, the money was gone, and so was my extra pair of glasses. So much for all that trusting.

Marilyn checked her suitcase—even though she had not been so silly as to stash money inside it—and found the zipper useless. Her loss was the damaged zipper as it was an expensive bag. I reported the theft and damage to Pam, who held a quick meeting to find out if anyone else had suffered a loss. There were only two of us if you didn't count Marilyn's zipper. Pam conferred with the Polish family who were the official chaperones on the trip. The family's oldest daughter was fluent in English and had a very sober and serious personality, at least when we dealt with her—already a power *pani*. The hotel owner became involved, and it was decided the police had to be called in.

Well, for some reason, Pam and I began to think everything was too hilarious, and we began laughing. Our laughter spread to a few of the others, but mainly Pam and I were the culprits. At one point, I was sitting beside the serious young translator on her bed and laughing while she scowled. I mentioned that it had been stupid to hide money in my suitcase, and she peered down her nose at me and finally said, "Yes."

Time passed, and someone called up the narrow staircase to our rooms that the police had arrived. Then I heard Ms. Serious call, "No laughing," in English. We all got straight and watched the approach of two young men dressed like snipers. With their black pants tucked into their boots, they looked forbidding, but they also looked like they might need to start shaving any day. They rattled our doorknob. We never locked the door because there were two people, but only one key. Then they frowned a lot and left. The keys were the old-fashioned kind we used to call skeleton keys—I think because they were as big and clunky as finger bones.

The next day the victims, with Pam and the translator, went to the police station to file a report while everyone else got to go ride the funicular and get a great view. We sat in a tile hallway on wooden chairs while male detectives in hard heeled shoes clacked briskly up and down to this and that office. Each time they came to a door, they would fish out a huge wad of keys from their pants pockets and noisily unlock the door, go in, and slam it behind them, almost as though they were pointing out the proper way to safeguard one's stuff. We finally entered an office behind one of these key-laden men and found lace curtains, potted spider plants, a desk, file cabinets, and a manual type-writer. The burly detective sat at the typewriter and pecked in Polish after we told Ms. Serious in English the answers to his questions in Polish. In the end, we were presented with a stack of papers, all in Pol-ish, that we needed to sign. We paused. Hadn't our parents always told us to read anything we signed? Then we signed, knowing full well that was the end of that.

Yet another learning experience as far as I was concerned. Carry your money and anything you don't want to lose with you. As soon as I could after the robbery, I e-mailed Wally from an Internet café, and his response was, "How can I help?" I told him all was well; I could get more money if I needed it at an ATM. Part of the reason I was not upset when I was robbed was that it was only money, OK, and glasses, but maybe someone could use the glasses. I have terrible eyes, and lenses like mine are greatly appreciated by people as near-sighted as I am. And it wasn't an amount of money that I couldn't afford to lose. I wouldn't take that much with me. And if laughing can lengthen your life, I must have gained at least a month on that trip. The laughing with Pam also cemented a friendship that has continued for years.

At the airport, on my way home, I was in for another travel lesson. My bag was already checked, but for some reason, I was rescheduled to leave the next morning. I was given a voucher for a room at a Warsaw hotel—very new, very modern, an American chain. I took a cab there and immediately set out to find the nearest Internet cafe to let Wally know I wouldn't be arriving when he thought I would. I was directed

to an underground section of the city, which was filled with shops, and the very railroad station Kathy and I had stumbled through on my first trip to Europe.

Internet cafés were always low-rent spaces filled with tables and chairs and computers. There could be as few as one computer, or there might be a dozen. The cafés were always staffed by young nerds. Café had nothing to do with it; they were for computer use only. In the U.S., so many people could afford their own computers, even in the early days, that there weren't many of these "cafés" around. A consistent problem was finding the pesky @ key. Foreign keyboards seemed to hide them. I would look and look for that little thing, and then finally draw it on a piece of paper and show it with an asking expression on my face to the person next to me or the nerd in charge.

In Zakopane, I went to the local Internet café one day and was turned away because it was filled with young boys who were having a gaming contest. I looked in, and sure enough, the place was filled with pencil necks, each top-heavy with giant headphones, concentrating and clicking away like they were running the world. By now, some of them probably are.

After letting Wally know I was delayed a day, I found some lunch and hit the desk clerk up for some needed toiletries. For dinner, I went to one of the fancy restaurants in the hotel and met a young woman who was stranded as I was. She was Polish but had moved to Canada, and we spoke in English. We agreed to dine together. I learned from her that I needed to see the airline people before my flight the next day to get reimbursed for my cab fares and dinner. I also learned the skinheads in Poland were still fanning the embers of the Nazi point of view—and not only with graffiti, but with violence. She told me she had considered emigrating to the United States but chose Canada for the free social services it offered once she became a citizen.

After dinner, we decided to walk around the block. There was a park behind the hotel, and here and there, beautiful, long-legged young women wearing glittery high heels, thigh-high skirts and practiced pouts, posed at the curb. After we passed them, we agreed they had

Opposite top: Countryside in the mountains of southern Poland. *Opposite bottom:* Country house and yard (courtesy Patty Carlson, Volunteer Relations Manager, Global Volunteers).

to be working girls. It made me wonder if the men in suits inside the hotel, men with coiled wires stretched between their collars and their ears, were hotel security or some level of "pimpage." It was all so glamorous and so sad. The women seemed to be the same age as the young women who had been my students. Perhaps some of them had grown up in towns like Zakopane, where family care was so broad it extended to the dead in their well-tended graves. It was a sad farewell from a place that felt so much like home.

4

Mexico,
Tequila and
Beer Ice Cream—
Age 61 (2004)

My flight was one that should have been listed under "you can't get there from here." To go south from Virginia, I had to go north to Chicago, then catch an Aeroméxico flight to León, then go on to Guanajuato. Europeans like to applaud a good landing; Mexicans add the sign of the cross. People were blessing themselves right and left as we took off and each time we landed. Although the plane had seen a lot of miles—judging from the tattered upholstery and the seat tray that would not stay in its locked and upright position—all that praying made me feel safe. I've been known to throw a few Hail Marys into the ascents and descents ever since that night flight when I had to toss my cookies into my gloves. This flight was smooth as silk compared with that one.

At Guanajuato, we met our roommates and stayed one night at a nice hotel, all done up in those bright Mexican colors—blue, yellow, red, green. The maid had turned the tissue box into a veritable bouquet of soft paper flowers, and the toilet paper was so nicely fanned on the roll that I paused a moment before tearing into it. If the décor hadn't signaled "foreign country," the menu did—rabbit. How often do you find that on the menu back home? It was a lovely pause for one night, and in the morning, we boarded a bus for Dolores Hidalgo.

Our digs at our destination were more modest than our first night's, but the décor was just as colorful, piñata style. You couldn't help but smile in an environment like that. Our shower liked to flood the bathroom floor, and the bed, when I plunked myself down, was far from "plunkable." I came up short with a thud: it was rigid. The door to our room was thin and ill fitting, the lock a loose hook-and-eye arrangement. A large cat could have shouldered the thing open. Neither my roommate—a middle-aged woman soon heading for a stint in the Peace Corps—nor I worried about our safety. Besides, I had learned in Zakopane not to leave valuables in my room. The important stuff was in a little pocket tied around my waist and cozied up to my underpants. We worked out a way to keep our feet dry after bathing and settled in.

Outside our window was a construction site. A building was going up with no power tools to speak of. Huge steel beams were hoisted with good old muscle power up the poorest excuse for a ladder I had ever seen. The unevenly spaced and crooked rungs didn't look like they could hold a chicken, much less a muscular man with part of a steel beam on his shoulder. Like the man in shorts and flip-flops I had seen running a jackhammer in Tahiti on a cruise with Wally, they seemed to know just what they were doing. No OSHA concerns here. If you fall down and kill yourself, well, it won't happen again, will it?

Dolores Hidalgo is a pleasant town famous for being the starting place of Mexico's revolution in 1810. The town is named for Miguel Hidalgo y Costilla, born 1753, a Roman Catholic priest and revolutionary. In 1803, he became the parish priest in Dolores. His flock was suspicious of him, as he went beyond his duties of celebrating Mass, baptizing, marrying, and burying the town's faithful. Perhaps he had too much education to be a simple parish priest. He had studied at a Jesuit secondary school and then earned a bachelor's degree in theology and philosophy. At any rate, he wanted to improve the economic situation for his people and offered them advanced ideas in agricultural methods, along with the gospel. To add tequila to the fire, he expressed his opinions about the Spanish oppression of the people. There was probably *mucho* muttering at the holy water font about that guy.

Now here's where the international politics come in. In 1808, Napoleon the First invaded Spain, booted King Ferdinand VII from his throne, and installed his brother Joseph Bonaparte as King of Spain. While it didn't seem prudent to go against the new king, some Mexicans thought they saw a glimmer of hope for independence and formed

Town square (courtesy Patty Carlson, Volunteer Relations Manager, Global Volunteers).

secret societies. Supporters of the new king did likewise, so you had to be sure of your secret handshake, or whatever you were using to identify the like-minded. Hidalgo trotted over to San Miguel (now San Miguel de Allende) and joined a pro-independence group. The Spanish got wind of this group and arrested some members. That's when Hidalgo decided to act and rang the church bell to gather the town people. His speech was about racial equality and land ownership, as well as a call to revolution. That speech became known as the Grito de Dolores or the Cry of Dolores.

From that event, Hidalgo became a leader of the revolt. The movement spread and became an upheaval of the lowest workers against the upper crust. Thousands of Indians and mestizos (mixed-race people) rallied, and Hidalgo led them under the banner of the Lady of Guadalupe to their war. He succeeded in taking Guanajuato (where we landed) and other cities but hesitated at the gates of the capital. That's when the tide turned against Hidalgo and his rebels, and Hidalgo fled north to the United States. Unfortunately, he was caught. History says he was expelled from the priesthood and executed by firing squad. Although he did not accomplish independence, Hidalgo's name became famous, and the anniversary of the Grito de Dolores (September 16) is now celebrated as Mexico's Independence Day.

Our team took meals in the hotel dining room and held our meetings around the table as well. On our first day at the community college campus, we were taken on a tour and met the teachers with whose students we would work. The building was tile, and the chairs and desks were metal. The noise when the students entered and left the classrooms was deafening. It was this trip that let me know my hearing loss was progressing quickly. The young men and women were eager to learn, and it was fun eating lunch with them in the shaded outdoor canteen. But, while I loved the beans, the beans did not love me. They did have Magnum ice cream bars, which I had never seen in the states and enjoyed.

Each morning after breakfast, we would head up the hill to the school, either on foot or by cab. Each day we came back down and walked through the town square, sampling ice cream and buying souvenirs. The ice cream vendors vie for the most exotic flavors, so there is shrimp, octopus, tequila, beer, avocado, and fried pork skin, among others.

The square was as lively at night as it was in the middle of the day. One of our team went out one evening and noticed a wedding at the church. Soon he found himself invited to dance with the bride, and he did. Children held their parents' hands and stared at another woman volunteer and me. One little boy smiled shyly and said to his mother, "Dos *gringas*, Mama," whereupon mama turned and smiled as well. Mariachi bands waited for engagement, their huge hats and guitars their only advertising. Is there anything sexier than those tight pants with the line of silver *conchos* running down a long, lean leg to a cowboy boot heel? Whoever topped that with a short jacket knew what they were doing. It works so well they still look *macho* in those girly ruffled shirts.

Circling the square, I was on the watch for cats, since I missed mine, but only spotted poor creatures flattened in the road. I had the impression that any beloved felines were locked up at home. The dogs were another story. While there were strays roaming for food, many drivers drove around town with their purebred pooches on their laps. I could only imagine the meaning of the woofs exchanged between the pampered and the poor at the stop sign—"Que pasa, flako?" from the one behind the wheel.

"Muerdeme, perra," from the flea-bitten one.

"What's up, skinny?"

"Bite me, bitch."

On the way to and from the college, we passed an elementary school. One day the kids were all outside in the courtyard. It seemed to be a celebration of something historic. They were all lined up, sort of, and wore bright red scarves around their necks. The little girls were decked out in long, ruffly skirts. There was trumpet music and vigorous stomping amongst the boys, while the girls stamped around flinging their skirts with such energy that you'd think they were infested with spiders. These are the kinds of sights and sounds that put a huge smile on my face and nary a thought of hauling out a camera. I see in words.

The Internet cafe was the usual interesting array of computers and boys and the occasional old lady traveler. This one was decorated with posters of singers, including Michael Jackson in full fro and a much darker skin shade than when he left us. This was a poster from before his voice changed, and I could almost hear him in that sweet, high-pitch singing, "You've got a friend." On the subject of posters, we were told that the U.S. took its "Got milk?" ad campaign to Mexico and ended up with a huge white mustachioed Michael Jordan asking, "Are you lactating?"

Of course, there was tequila. It was so good that I nodded a "thank you" every time I recognized the agave cactus from which it's made. The hotel restaurant served drinks. That is, you told the owner you wanted a Margarita, and he went back to the kitchen and brought it out and handed it to you. Then one night, we met to discuss some team matters, and the hotel owner announced we would be served a special treat, courtesy of the hotel. This was something-something, Guadalajara style. It was a little glass bowl with fresh fruit and a cold liquid. We were provided both spoons and straws. I was not the only one who thought it was soup and dug in. It turned out to be heavily laced with tequila, and we were all slurping our bowls empty by the end of that pleasant meeting.

On the weekend, we took a bus to San Miguel de Allende, a beautiful town discovered by a lot of Americans long after Padre Hidalgo honed his revolutionary zeal there. Our bus driver, seen from the side, was the perfect image of the Aztec profiles incised on bowls in museums. He was a beautiful, finely boned young man. A huge metal watch hung loose on his fine wrist. That evening, we dined in a fancy restaurant's courtyard. There were so many tequilas that it was difficult to know what to select. Some of us chose to order it straight and were brought a chaser of what seemed a liquid salsa. Tasted alone, this drink was spicy hot; taken after the tequila, it was perfect.

At one point, I sat back in my carved wooden chair and looked up into the night sky, which was framed by the adobe walls of the courtyard. I imagined a movie scene in which we were suddenly surrounded by sombrero-topped, bandolier-strapped, mustachioed *banditos*, coming over the wall with their rifles. Weren't there at least fifty movies with that scene back in the day?

One day, we boarded a bus and went to a school in the country, similar to the one where we were working. We met the teachers and students and then were seated in a classroom where the students presented a play they had written. It was about a young man who decided he would cross the border to the U.S. and how he died in the desert and how his family grieved for him. It was an expression of frustration, and we found ourselves unable to comment but merely telling the students how well they had performed. As Americans, we were the villains; as their guests, we kept our thoughts to ourselves.

After that, we were introduced to a local dance, with young men and women in costume stepping hard and loud on the classroom floor. After our applause, the music began again, and a young man came to ask me to dance. I couldn't refuse, and so I hopped and stamped as best I could with him, along with all the other volunteers and students.

On the ride to the airport at the end of this trip, I thought about the students and how mature they seemed and how hard they were working on getting ahead. Out of the bus window, I enjoyed the blooming jacaranda trees and was happy I had answered the urge to get out of town. I also made a mental note to have my hearing checked—

someday soon—avoid beans for a while, and look harder for Magnum ice cream bars. I would probably get some tequila at the liquor store when I got back as well.

As for the students' play, it was the very kind of experience to come from a volunteering vacation. It gave me more to think about than I believe I would have had returning from a tour.

5

Hungary,
Cold Nights and
Public Laundry—
Age 61 (2004)

The year 2004 saw me heading off on two trips alone. Spring in Mexico—and then fall found me heading for Hungary to teach English once more for Global Volunteers with young adults in a vocational school. I chose to cash in some frequent flyer miles and booked business class and also sprang for the extra fee to have a private room. The business class decision would turn out to be even more accommodating than usual on my return.

Before I left, I had lunch with a Hungarian friend who let me know the language is unlike any other Western language I might be familiar with. It is a Uralic or Finno-Ugric language, and the most closely related languages are Mansi and Khanty of Western Siberia. I could see this would be a lingual experience close to visiting, oh, I don't know, China, but with a familiar alphabet.

Hungary sent a lot of intellectuals to the West when they fled the revolution back in the 1950s and later. The government took its time settling down, and except for Budapest, that marvelous city that claims so many world visitors, other parts seemed still to be in economic recovery.

The Mexican students had been about the same age as the students in these classes, but the demeanor was different. Maybe it was all that sunshine and warm weather in Mexico—or the tequila—but the Mexican students seemed more carefree, happier. Hungary was dark and cool; winter was on its way. People wore dark leather jackets and somber-colored clothing. They smoked and were serious as they went about their business. It reminded me of the beatnik look I affected as an English major in the Sixties: black turtleneck and stockings, leather skirts, cigarettes and poetry. See me, the intellectual, and how I'm suffering for my art. Leave me alone while I brood like a surly hen.

The hotel was an interesting place, as usual, not fancy. The staff was small, and you might see a person all dressed up for desk clerk duty heading to your room with toilet cleaning kit in hand. They would do laundry for a fee, so some of us tried that. I sent some blouses, and they were returned to my room, ironed, and hung neatly in my closet while I was out. We found out they were drying the clothes on racks in the courtyard when one of the men on the team walked through and recognized his underwear flapping in the breeze.

My room was small and had a complete bath. There were windows that overlooked a slanted roof, and most importantly, there was a good reading lamp by the bed. It was, however, quite cold at night, and I piled on the blankets, duvet, whatever I had. Pam was again our leader, and she took herself off to see the mayor about the matter. As in other Eastern European countries to which I had traveled, the town had one big heating system, and it was too early to turn it on, according to the rules. Pam had them turn it on, and we were grateful. I always wondered if she made some kind of contribution to the town coffers. I know our fees helped the programs in which we participated. Perhaps she gently reminded him of that. At any rate, my hand-washed undies now dried overnight on the radiator, and I stopped wearing a wool hat to bed.

Pam enjoyed finding restaurants that had interesting meals for us to select. Lunching at a restaurant near our hotel, we began with soup, which was followed by mashed potatoes with fish on top. The dessert was a chocolate pudding with bread, topped with whipped cream and chocolate syrup. After a few more of these enormous meals, we pleaded for either soup or dessert, but not both. My favorite soup was a cold cherry soup. My least favorite was carp soup, served, one night, in a clever red metal pail. I tasted a few spoonfuls and was having a hard time. Finally, I put my spoon down, and a waiter immediately appeared and gestured that he could remove the soup. I nodded, and the bowl was, to my surprise, quickly replaced with a one of cold cherry soup. You gotta love professional waitering. That was one of the skills being taught at the school where we worked. The school also trained young men and women in such things as working in shops, a job that required an identifying jacket or smock.

The classrooms were decorated with posters featuring scantily clad, provocatively posed rock stars. And yet, the students all seemed so serious. The place was large, and changing classes was sometimes a trek. We met with classes and conducted casual conversation groups. They wanted to know the meaning of things like "pimp my ride." One of the young men, in a leather jacket, serious as an old-school librarian, had a zippered pencil bag with that image of Einstein with his tongue out. I asked him where he got it, and he said his mother had bought it and he would find out. Then one day on the street, he saw me and told me where she had bought it. What made this entire business odd was, like the other students in the school, he did not appear in the least like a pupil. If you lifted them as they were and plunked them down in New York City, they would appear to be young adults with jobs, families, and rent to pay—all the usual accoutrements of adulthood. No hint of school about them. Yet, his mother bought him a pencil case as she probably did when he was in the first grade. Thanks to him, I now pack my crochet hooks in a Hungarian, Einstein-decorated pencil case.

At lunchtime, we were given tickets to use in the cafeteria. One of the teachers accompanied another volunteer and me and explained what was on the menu. The serving was handled by large women wearing white aprons and white caps. The food was in large metal vats, and the women had enormous metal ladles and the arms to wield them. I was reminded of the black-and-white films I was shown in grade school, the ones with female Russian workers with forearms like Popeye. The meal always included bread, juice, and dessert. It was the main course that one needed to identify because it was served in bowls the size of basins. If you didn't like it, a lot of food would be wasted. We watched tiny kids, maybe six years old and a bit on the frail side, carry trays laden with these bowls and the rest of their lunch. They would carefully get to a table, sit down, and methodically consume every bite. One day, the main course was tripe, and my volunteer partner relished it. Never having had it, I declined, but I did taste his, and it was good.

5. *Hungary, Cold Nights and Public Laundry*

One weekend, a group of us went to the Ópusztaszer Historical Park, about an hour outside of town. We viewed the Feszty Panorama, a cyclorama depicting the arrival of the Hungarians to the Carpathian Basin in 895 CE. It was a spiraling diorama exhibit in which we walked up a slightly inclined ramp. In addition to this, we watched re-enactors in costume and on horseback demonstrate ancient fighting techniques around the park. Pam warned us that the head of the park would be asking us for ideas on how to get tourists to come to the place. All we could offer was what we had learned in the United States: people will only pay for these things if they have expendable money or they can borrow it. The people we were meeting seemed to be in a category that did not fit. Too bad one of us wasn't an economist who could really explain things.

Pam and I had brought knitting and went shopping one evening in a small yarn shop. Most of the stuff was behind the counter on shelves, so Pam went right back there and started pulling things off the shelves. The clerk was alarmed, but Pam reassured her in English, which the woman didn't seem to understand, that we would buy these things. Apparently, it worked. The woman watched carefully but no longer objected as we made our selections. We paid, and everyone was happy. Pam could take care of business and not offend.

Although the town struck me as cold and dark with heavy stone structures everywhere, the architecture was magnificent, especially that of the city hall. That's where we had a meeting with the mayor. It was like Versailles inside, and we received gift bags. They were heavy, and we were hoping it was a bottle of wine. Instead, it contained a lovely picture book and a CD of Liszt performances.

The second weekend, my final one, was spent in Budapest with some members of the group plus Pam. We toured the city and visited museums. At dinnertime, we piled into a cab and gave the driver the name of a restaurant to which we wanted to go. He drove this way and that, and some of us thought perhaps we were being taken for a ride, if you know what I mean. Pam asked him if he spoke English (in English).

He said, "No," in English.

She said, "Right."

Our doubts strengthened. We knew we had been taken when, after dinner, we came out of the restaurant and approached a cab with the address of our hotel. This driver looked at us kind of funny when he read the address and was trying to refuse us, but we assured him we wanted to ride in his cab. He took us halfway around the block and delivered us to our destination. Case closed.

On Saturday, after the others left to go back for the third week of teaching, which I wasn't doing, I stayed on at the hotel for one more night. That Sunday was lovely. I walked and looked, sent some e-mails that made my name appear as "Judz" because of the strange keyboard, then settled into a café full of little sitting areas with sofas and coffee tables. There I enjoyed food and drink, read and wrote. It was a great way to wind down. It gave me time to think about my experiences and realize that volunteer teaching was really quite stressful for me. I think I had convinced myself that because I had once been a teacher, I needed to continue as a volunteer. I could try other kinds of work. As for my physical abilities, I had followed our octogenarian volunteer up the stairs in a church tower and thought she seemed more energetic than I. Hmm.

All went well on the return flights, or did it? I fell asleep on the first leg of the trip, between Budapest and Paris, and woke on landing. The flight attendant was telling me I would be the first person off the plane and was hauling out my carryon bag for me. I wondered what this was about. The door opened, and I saw a man in a safety vest and other runway gear at the bottom of the stairs to the tarmac holding a sign with a badly spelled version of my name on it. I went down, and he hustled me into a van. Then we tore around the tarmac this way and that. He screeched to a halt, jumped out with my bag and hustled me into the terminal and to the bottom of a people-free escalator. Standing there was a tiny young Asian woman with a suitcase and a baby. My escort looked at her and asked where she was going. She said Vietnam. He grabbed her bag, too, and we all went rushing up the escalator, which wasn't working. Not far from the top, he ushered me into a line of people boarding a plane, handed me the bag, and rushed off with the young woman and her child.

On the dash over in the van, my driver told me that I would have made my connection if the plane hadn't landed twice. Twice? Apparently, I had slept through one landing. The plane then had to take off—to avoid a collision—and come around again. Having been through

Charles de Gaulle airport a number of times, I knew it took at least an hour to get from one terminal to another. My escort got me to my connection, and I was grateful. Lesson learned—if the flying is going to be frightening, it's better to be asleep. Also, they go the extra mile if you ride up front.

6

Greece,
Doing What I Couldn't Do—
Age 62 (2005)

Having not enjoyed the teaching I did in Hungary, particularly—the ex-teacher in me wanted order and insisting on it was only making me miserable—I decided to look into other sorts of volunteer work. I came across another Global Volunteer program, this one with severely disabled people in northern Greece. I knew nothing about the severely disabled, was never much of a nurse type, and avoided—as many of us do—even looking at such people when I rarely saw them. But, once again, Pam was the leader and had done it before. In a phone call, she assured me I could handle the experience. Pam was very good at matching up roommates. This time she put me with Ellen, and it was a perfect match. We are still friends. I flew into Thessaloniki, where I met the five other team members and Pam. We then took two cabs, in tight NASCAR formation, through the pine-forested hills to Sidderokastro, a trip that took an hour or so.

This team consisted of veterans of the Global Volunteers program, so we all felt comfortable that everyone would settle right into the rules of being good ambassadors and willing learners and workers. Experienced volunteer vacationers tend to be happy, patient, understanding, flexible, open-minded, strong, obedient, thrifty, and, of course, good-looking and above average. After quickly dumping our luggage in our rooms, then meeting one of our Greek hosts, we were off to dinner at a restaurant, where I encountered my first-ever squat toilet. Talk about a place that needs handicap rails. Of course, there weren't any. The walk back to the hotel revealed a lot about the local culture we would be enjoying in the next couple of weeks. Families were out and about, people sat at sidewalk cafes, men played backgammon, and the whole pleasant scene was stitched together by zipping cars and motorbikes—motorbikes that seemed cheerfully unencumbered by mufflers. One of our group members loved every stray pup she encountered as they cruised the café tables. As we walked, Pam pointed out essential services: the ATM at the bank, the pastry shop, phones, a pastry shop, phone card vendors, pastry shops, pastry shops, and more pastry shops. Needless to say, some of us stopped and sampled pastries, which were not only tasty but works of culinary art.

After breakfast the first morning, we learned more about our host country. As there was not a tradition of volunteerism, handicapped people were cared for in the homes of their relatives. Every day, we learned more about the culture, some of it handed to us by our leader, some observed. For instance, a Greek man at a coffee shop always had these items at hand: cigarettes, lighter, cell phone, and worry beads. Some of this education came by experience. One night, I discovered I had left my purse in the restaurant where we had dinner. I knocked on Pam's door, and the two of us headed out into the almost vacant streets, in our end-of-the-day comfortable clothes. The restaurant was still open, and my purse had been moved from the chair where I had left it to the coat rack. Not a thing was missing.

On Monday, we boarded a bus and went up the hill to visit the institution where the people we would work with lived. The place opened in 1979 and housed 56 disabled people, referred to as "children." Ages ranged from ten months to 42 years. As we were about to enter the plain masonry building, Pam turned to us and asked pleasantly if we knew that breathing through our mouths might be an advantage. She then turned and, without hesitation, headed for the entrance. I was not the only one already spooked by what we were about to see, and this didn't help. We already knew the people we would work with could not speak, wore diapers, and could not walk. Now we knew the place would smell like an institution that housed diapered people. Pam moved us quickly through the door. No more time to dread; time to find out. Inside we saw some mobile residents who could speak, but, of course, they were speaking Greek, and there were ambulatory people who cared not to speak. One of these was a muscular young man with dark hair and heavy brows, who was particularly good at slamming the big heavy metal doors wherever he went. We soon called him the doorman. He went up to an open door and hauled off with enough power to knock out a horse. We heard the clang whether we were inside or outside the building. I realized I knew nothing. I had never considered I might encounter strong, uncommunicative adults like him. Eyes wide, breathing through our mouths, we were taken to an office to chat with an English-speaking member of the administration and one of the aides. There were two "children" as well. These were men, fully clothed in sweatpants and shirts, seated on the floor. One was much taller than the other. Neither spoke. As we listened to the administrator and learned more about the facility, we calmly watched and did not watch the men. Both sat with their feet spread out, the smaller one in the V created by the taller one's legs. As the smaller man sat and fumbled with an object in front of him, the larger man would wrap his arms around the smaller man and pull him closer in a bear hug.

I attempted a little conversation with the English-speaking aide who had accompanied the men. I asked her if she had been to the United States. She said no and that she did not like the United States. That served as a reminder that good behavior on my part was essential and that my country is not the center of the universe—even though that volunteer in Poland seemed to indicate it might be. Or, maybe it was, and that was the problem. Either way, I needed to zip it.

After that, we met the director, who took us on a limited tour and explained that certain individuals had been selected to be brought down to the town's community center each day, and we would go there to work with them. An aide would be sent with the people and help us a little.

Two of our group would be working with a group of regular citizens who wanted to learn English. Four of us would be working with the severely disabled. On the first morning at the recreation center, our charges arrived in a van, and each volunteer simply went up the ramp one at a time and claimed a person. Ellen had a woman in her 20s so small she fit into a child's stroller. She could not speak and simply curled inward. I had a young woman in her 20s also, but she was different from the others. She was of normal size and rode in a huge wheelchair sort of recliner built to accommodate her twisted form. She could actually make eye contact but was shy and would not look at me that first day. Two weeks later, we would be laughing. She won my heart, and I dreamed about her that night.

With the help of the aides and others in the program, we learned to play music and engage the "children" with the tunes. There were mats on the floor, and we could get them down onto them and move their limbs to the music. We also wheeled them outside and up the street to the park. My charge, Vasula, revealed charming dimples when I finally was able to make her smile. Trust me, the antics I went through were a workout, just to get that little grin. I jumped and danced and smiled and sang, but I was careful not to touch her as that sent her into her shell. One day, we decided to take them through the market so that their fellow citizens could see them. Surely they knew there were disabled people up on the hill. Now they could actually see some of them. I had bought a pink baseball cap to keep the sun from Vasula's eyes, and she looked like a grim tourist as I wheeled her through the street. She was not amused. Ellen had bought a hat for her girl as well, but she was able to swing her tiny arms and fling it from her head.

One afternoon, for a break, we visited the nunnery on the hill that we could see from our hotel window. The nuns wore full habits the way nuns did in the fifties in the U.S., with floor-length white skirts, full sleeves, veils and wimples. They ushered us into a pretty little parlor and then rushed out and back in with tiny cups of coffee, each with a small perfect cookie on the saucer. There was no chitchat. They were on the run like they had skates on under those skirts—things to do, souls to save, busy, busy. We enjoyed seeing the mosaics and embroideries, which take years to complete, that they make. Then we were sent home. On the walk back, I found money along the road. Ellen and I picked up Euro coins all over the place. No way to find out who might have flung them there.

Like other traditionally Catholic countries, Greece has shrines along the road. These were little buildings about the size of four or five combined phone booths, if you can remember them. Inside, there were icons, hanging censors for votive lights and incense, maybe a table with tablecloth, certainly curtains and fake flowers, and behind the door in one of them—cleaning supplies. I would enter them and light candles for my departed loved ones and leave some coins. I had plenty.

Cat in an older hillside neighborhood.

One day, Vasula was not in the van when it arrived at the rec cen-ter. I asked the aide about her, and she tried to explain that Vasula was suffering from some ailment, not serious, and would be back the next day. In the meantime, they had brought Nikos for me. Nikos was not only a man who could walk: he could speak Greek, liked to cuddle

An embroidered priest's chasuble, exquisitely hand stitched by nuns we visited (courtesy Ellen Westbrook).

dolls, and loved to go to the movies. If I had seen this man on the street at any other place and time, I would have tried not to stare and would certainly have avoided contact. He was bristly-bearded, his hair ran amok, and, like all the others, his teeth were a smelly disaster. He also had a peculiar gait and manner.

Away we went to a table because he liked to draw. I soon found out that there wasn't enough paper and there weren't enough crayons in the entire town to keep him drawing all morning. His art and process consisted of two seconds of scribbling with a crayon, a proud waving of the paper, and a pantomimed demand to have it hung on the wall. As soon as we used up the paper (after about two minutes), we tossed a ball, went for a walk, examined a burro tied up in the yard next door, and passed our time.

Another day, we went up the hill at lunchtime and fed our children. Vasula was able to eat from a spoon I held to her mouth. Ellen, a nurse, kindly instructed how to do it—stand a little to one side, not directly in front. The food, a slurry of something smelling like supper, was in a large metal bowl. She also drank juice from a cup. The others were not so fortunate. Their food was presented in baby bottles with large holes cut in the nipples. They did not suck the food out, but gnawed on the soft tops and swallowed greedily. Since none of them could use their hands, we volunteers provided the input. It became even clearer how these people were at the mercy of their caretakers. There simply was no food, no liquid for them unless someone prepared it, brought it, and put it into their mouths. I carefully tried to gauge how rapidly to spoon the warm gruel into Vasula's mouth so that I would satisfy but not choke her.

Ellen and our only male volunteer had begun going up the hill after lunch to continue working with our people. I went one day and was introduced to the room that was spread with padded mats and scattered with large toys. We took off our shoes and got down on the mat with them and had at it—all to the accompanying sounds of slamming doors, thanks to the doorman who was roaming the area. It sounded like freight cars coupling. We were much more at ease than we had been that first day when we had entered with open mouths and roaming eyes.

Then came the evening of the big-deal party. We dolled up as best we could—a scarf here, some special earrings there—and went up the hill, where, to our surprise, the press had assembled. We were seated beside the bigwig platform facing the folk singers and dancers. A variety of VIPs and others (a lot of suits and at least one military uniform) were stuffed into the room with us, along with photographers, television crews and several of our children. We feared the last might be crushed. There was much grand speaking, handshaking, and smiling, and there were many camera lights. We were recognized one by one and received big medals on ribbons— just like the Olympics—and a gift bag with books, worry beads and a calendar book illustrated with children's art. Then a stream of dignitaries spoke and traded awards, medals, etc. Then the folk singers sang, and then we dispersed. As we didn't know who was who during the shindig, it was astonishing to shake hands with one of the Greek-speaking presenters and hear him reply in perfect Midwestern USA English—a diplomat.

Then it was off to our favorite restaurant, the one where I had left my purse: musicians and dancers, babies and children, dignitaries and us. We all chowed down on plenty of great food and drank little bottles of wine made from the earliest grapes—wine served in small glasses for good reason, it turned out. Soon the Greek flutes and drum started up, and the dancers danced, the drinkers drank, and the building seemed to tremble. The Greek flute's sound was at least the same decibel as the horn on a semi—no, actually twice as loud. I stuffed my ears with bits of tissue, drank more wine, and then got up and danced with a woman in a costume of layers; skirt, apron, blouse, vest, scarves, head dress. You name it, she was wearing it. At one point, we held hands and bending backward, away from each other, spun in a circle. If the wine didn't nail me then, it wasn't going to. The party ended when we danced our way out into the street. Thank goodness I didn't eat and drink so much that I couldn't stop at a pastry shop on the way back to the hotel. Back in the room, I was certain the flutes had made me deaf. I was becoming annoyed that I had traveled all this way to do what I hoped was good work, and it cost me my hearing, #*@&. Then I dug out the last of the tissue. What a relief, no more deaf than usual.

On weekends, we went off touring. One Saturday, we piled into a large bus and headed for Thessaloniki. That was the day the weather decided to turn from sunny and delightful to as wet as it could get. Once in the city, Ellen and I veered off on our own and wandered through all kinds of neighborhoods to the Museum of Byzantine Culture and the harbor where the rain drove sideways into us, and the waves blew through the air behind it. The color of the water brought back Homer's phrase "wine-dark seas," and I wondered again if the Mediterranean was red or purple back in those days or the wine a blue-grey color.

At one point, we wandered into the city's own Hagia Sophia, an ancient church modeled on the one in Constantinople. We were just in time to watch a child's baptism. The women were dressed to kill, with heels like daggers. The child was naked and had a lock of hair cut off; then a funny hat was placed on his head. It must have been the day for baptisms because we shortly came upon another, this one with little toys and favors for the guests. I enjoyed a little combustion time in that church by lighting more candles for my dearly departed.

When it was time to head for the bus station, we began hailing cabs and, of course, they were all filled because of the rain. Finally, we spotted a very nice hotel and, with squishing shoes, made our way across the marble lobby to request the concierge get us a cab. It arrived, and off we went, time dwindling. Once at the station, we ran from bus to bus, looking at their destination signs and finding nothing for Sidderokastro. Because I couldn't pronounce it, I kept showing my ticket to the drivers, who seemed to have never heard of it. Then, right after the driver had started the engine, we found our bus and climbed aboard. I grabbed a seat, pulled off my shoes and socks, and squeezed out the water and put them on the heater. Then I fished out the dry socks I had cleverly stashed in my pack, put them on, and propped my feet on the heater as well. Ahhhh. If getting older means getting smarter, I thought, bring it on.

Another weekend day found us wandering the archeological ruins of Philippi. As we listened to our guide and took pictures of the ruins, I kept thinking, "How do I know this place?" Then I remembered the priest at church announcing that he would read us a letter from St. Paul to the Philippians. This very spot on the earth where I was standing was where those Philippians lived and may have heard the letter read to them, perhaps even touching this scrap of building, pushing up through the grasses, at which I stared. The first walls were erected in 356 BCE. Then, a mere 314 years later in 42 BCE, the rock star Roman senators Brutus and Cassius went into battle against Octavian (later known as Augustus Caesar) and Mark Antony. The defeat of Brutus and Cassius by the men who had assumed power after Caesar's death changed the Roman Republic into the Roman Empire. Then Christ came and went, and St. Paul arrived in 49 CE and established the first Christian church in Europe. This kind of history made my American head spin. No one came along and started fighting over our resources for 1,400 years or so, give or take a theory as to whether that person was an Italian or a Norseman. My foot was poking at someone's wall or temple or brothel from before Americans considered piling stone for shelter. Once, this was part of the greatest power on earth. So much to think about.

Then there was the pre-dining experience with Pam. As noted before, she liked to find interesting restaurants for us to dine in, and she had her eye on one that was through the town and on the other side of a little bridge. She invited me to walk over there one evening to check it out. The place had plenty of customers, and we walked up to the counter, where she began to ask questions in English. No one spoke English, but she plowed ahead. In the meantime, she told me to find out what was good, and I opened a menu, looked through it, and then

Ruins in Philippi. St. Paul sent a letter to the enclave of Christian converts that he established here around 52 CE (courtesy Ellen Westbrook).

Ellen in doorway of the ruins at Philippi.

mentally gave myself a nice big dope slap. I couldn't read it, of course. She said, "No, no, go around and look at people's plates and ask." Now that wasn't going to happen, and I stayed at the counter while she went into the kitchen where someone handed her a phone with an English speaker on the other end of the line. She successfully set up dinner for our group for the next night, and then she and I sat down, and I ordered a glass of *ouzo* because I had never had it. Neither one of us liked it, so it remained on the table when we left.

Soon our last day arrived, and it was my best time with Vasula. By now, she didn't mind my touch. It happened at the playground. I sat in a swing and would sweep towards her in her chair, tapping the arms with my feet. She loved it, smiling widely. I also picked up small stones and would put one in her hand and then carry her hand and arm in mine; together, we threw it as hard as we could. I'll bet she never did that before. I doubt she has done it since. I think of her often and wonder if she ever sees the light of day unfiltered by windows or if she is still alive other than in my memory.

Something very important happened on that trip. I discovered, as another volunteer put it, that I was "able to do what I could not do."

7

Romania,
Falling in Baby Love—
Age 63 (2006)

On September 11, 2006, I saw a baby named Vasily in his crib at a Failure-to-Thrive Clinic in Tutova, Romania. He was just one of five infants in a room full of cribs. The room had masonry walls, tile floors and high ceilings. The cribs were against the walls, end to end, and took up all the wall space in the room. There was one window. The children were of different ages. Purely at random, I walked to Vasily's crib, where he lay quietly, a rash reddening one cheek, and picked him up. Little did I know he would break my heart.

For two weeks, I was part of a team of Global Volunteers at a hospital clinic in Tutova, a rural community 12 miles south of Barlad—a city of 80,000 people close to the Moldovan border in eastern Romania. Since the revolution in 1989, Romania (and Barlad in particular) had gone through many changes—some positive and some negative. There had been many layoffs and little to no education at all with regard to family planning. These factors led to even more child abandonment than before the revolution. We were there to provide a little attention to these children.

The hospital had three sections: an adult ward, a pediatric section, and the Failure-to-Thrive Clinic for children between birth and three years. We worked with the children in the clinic. The children were brought there by their families or sent there by the Children's Hospital from Barlad for medical reasons. Their main problem was that they could not maintain a healthy weight because of their own poor nutrition or the poor nutrition of their mothers during pregnancy.

They usually arrived when they were three or four months old. Parents simply did not have enough food for them, and sometimes they left their children in the clinic for years. Children went back to their families when they recovered. However, if the parents could not take them home because of poverty, the children went to foster families or were adopted. Parents or guardians had to agree to the adoption. There were, however, children in a sort of limbo. Simply abandoned, these children had no birth certificates, and so they did not officially exist. If you do not exist, you cannot be adopted, even though you are right there with one finger in your mouth looking like hope itself.

Our job was to help the children develop as normally as possible. To that end, we took them out of their cribs and played with them and helped them crawl, walk, eat, and interact with each other. At other times, we simply held and cuddled them. Actually, there was a lot of that. When volunteers were not on site, the children stayed in their cribs. The Romanian staff at the hospital were loving and caring people, but there was only one doctor for all three sections of the hospital and only one nurse and two aides per shift in the Failure-to-Thrive Clinic. It's all they could do to bathe, dress, change (every four hours) and feed 27 children—and also to clean the place, to cook all the food, to wash all the diapers, clothes and bedding and line dry it, plus to keep some records on the condition of each child. That is why the children were not potty-trained or taught to brush their teeth. While there was a playground outside and there were strollers in the hallway, the amount of work precluded much, if any, use of these when volunteers weren't there.

Each day we arrived around 9:00 a.m. Although Vassily was mine to concentrate on, we needed to help each other as well. That's how I learned I could sit on the floor and, with a bit of leg-pretzeling, feed two or three babies at a time. We started out with five infants and five volunteers just for them. Soon two volunteers from our group were called out to help with the special-needs children. In the second week, one of the volunteers went home (she was scheduled to only work one week). Two more of us left after two weeks. That left two volunteers with five babies, and a new baby arrived during the final week of the team's term.

The babies had a range of problems. Vassily and his twin brother,

Daniel, six months old, were born prematurely and hydrocephalic. In addition, their 17-year-old mother did not have enough breast milk, so they were put on cow's milk, causing severe diarrhea. Poor Daniel had returned from hernia surgery just before we arrived. Both boys had flat, narrow heads from too much crib time, and their necks were weak so that their heads flopped to one side consistently. These were not serious problems, and there are, no doubt, children in the U.S. like this, but I had not seen any. So, like the emotional jolt from the industrial doors clanging at the institute in Greece, where my dear Vasula lived, the little shock to my innocence soon evaporated. It happened as soon as those little eyes met mine.

We went to the clinic for a visit the day before we started work. For a short time, it was overwhelming. Yes, there was a smell greeting you at the door. It was an institution with industrial cleaning odors, and—let's face it—dirty diapers stink, especially in quantity. Then there were the rooms with six cribs in each and the communal changing area in the hallway. There was some crying here and there for whatever reason. But the halls and rooms were painted with bright flowers and storybook characters, and the children were all well-dressed and clean and had plenty of toys available.

We had four volunteers returning to work at the clinic. One man had been there eight times. A couple had been there four times. They had worked with babies and had seen them progress through toddlerhood to foster homes. These veterans went looking for children they knew and were smiling and swinging kids overhead in no time at all. It was obvious the children were delighted to see them and ran to them with arms raised to be picked up. Following their lead, we spread out and started picking kids at random. That's when I found my little love.

The next day was our first real day at work. Those of us working with the infants brought them from their cribs to a room with walls brightly painted with Disney characters and a floor laid with equally bright quilts. It was apparently the work of former volunteers, as so many of them tend to be American. I looked little Vasily in the eye and told him that by the time I left his little head would be upright and not always diving to starboard.

I fed Vassily (and others) a bottle at 9:00 a.m. in the little room.

We had little seats in which to park them if we had our hands full. This bottle contained some kind of orange stuff, which I think was ground-up carrots and broth. The youngest baby got formula. Then we just played with them and got them to do things they wouldn't do if they were lying in their cribs, like move around on their tummies—or, in the case of the twins, stretch their necks in the direction opposite to the one it wanted to go. At about 11:30, they brought us yogurt, which was actually the leftover (unopened) containers served to us at breakfast at the hotel. Two or three bowls, two spoons, and we figured it out. Then at noon, we put the babies into their cribs. There were diaper changes in between. Normally, the children were all changed on schedule, but the volunteers were out there wiping butts constantly. I believe there was some competition for greatest number of diapers or grossest load changed in a day or the speediest change. I refrained and even contributed to the effort by handing babies over for their needs. At the end of my stay, I actually changed a few diapers, and thank goodness no one got hurt. They used cloth diapers, of course. Each child was double-diapered. It didn't matter if you were two months old or two years old, you got two yards of fabric pinned around your bottom and between your little legs. The pins were next to impossible to get through the cloth. Some were rusty—even though I personally brought a pound or so of new ones.

All the children went to bed at noon, whether they wanted to or not. I lingered for a moment after I put Vassily in his crib one day and watched a toddler scoot to the head of her crib and rhythmically commence banging her head. I headed off to lunch with the same quiet space in my head that I had when I'd met the penned wolves when I was seven on that trip to Canada. One day, we had spotted a roadside attraction—See the Wild Wolves. We paid our money and were directed to a path that led through the woods. We trooped back there, single file, and arrived at a chain-link fenced enclosure a bit smaller than a single-car garage. There were some wood shelters—sort of dog houses—inside, and the wolves were in there, minding their business, silent, serious as blizzards. Two of them were pacing the inside perimeter with an evenness of step that was eerie. Their paws had formed a groove in the packed earth of the pen. Our presence had no effect on the determined walking and the lost gaze of the animals. We returned

Baby bottle in water-damaged wood box on the changing table.

to the car as silent as the wolves. If you can't pace, you can at least bang your head to know you exist.

We had lunch at a picnic table on the grounds. The food was prepared by the project leader's mother and consisted of homemade soup and a main dish, bread, and bottled water. The team leader made sure we always had big chocolate bars to share for dessert. A small pack of dogs waited patiently for us to finish. Any Romanians in the area would speak quietly to these dogs, and they would simply turn tail and saunter away.

7. *Romania, Falling in Baby Love*

The children's naptime ended at 2:00 p.m., so many of us went walking along the dirt road and down the village streets until then. My roommate Ellen, whom I met on my previous Global Volunteers trip in Greece, wanted to ride on one of the many horse-drawn carts on the road. So, one day, she simply stepped into the road when one was approaching. When the man driving stopped, she petted the horse and said how beautiful he was. It didn't hurt that she's a tall, willowy blonde. The next thing I knew, Ellen had hoisted herself effortlessly onto the sacks of grain on the wagon, but try as I might, I wasn't able to get up there. With some help, I was soon sitting on the seat next to a weathered Romanian who handed me the reins. These were heavy leather straps, satiny with wear. I yelled what he yelled at the horse, and away we went. Ellen sat in the back on the sacks of grain. We were able to convey what our work was—"'ospital" translated and a cradling motion with the arms said the rest. We were dropped off at the door, and when I extended my hand for shaking, it was kissed. A stubble beard and hands like leather, a little gift for crossing the ocean.

One day while I was there, Vasily's and Daniel's parents visited. An aide rushed into the infant room, speaking Romanian and carrying small homemade quilts. She was reaching for the babies and for me, and I caught one word I could understand. It was "Gemini," and I knew she wanted the twins. We bundled the boys and took them to the fragrant entrance. There I handed Vasily over to his mother, and the aide gave Daniel to his father. The poor parents looked stunned. When we went back to collect the babies, their father was kissing them goodbye. They were an attractive couple. He was blonde, and she brunette—thus the difference in the boys' big brown and blue eyes.

The next day after lunch, our adventure was of a knitting persuasion. We came upon three women patients sitting on a bench on the hospital grounds, and one was knitting, so I whipped my little baby hat project out of my backpack, and they jumped up to examine it. There was much discussion, during which I could tell they figured out the pattern and indicated I might want to consider using circular needles—either that or something about the European Union, I wasn't sure. Then we took pictures. They all smoothed their hair, retied their headscarves, and adjusted their bathrobes. We went back to work clouded by the idea that they may have had tuberculosis.

At two o'clock each day, we plucked the babies from their cribs and fed them bottles of formula—well, actually a mixture of tea, cooked flour and water for thickener, and formula. The children were all chubby, but I'm not sure of the nutritional value of their meals. Burping was expedited by Vasily's echoing belch. The others seemed to want to rise to the precedent. Then we would take them outside and cuddle or wheel them around in strollers or park them on a blanket among assorted mobile infants, or crawlers, and special-needs children.

In the meantime, toddlers toddled, some inside the cage, AKA playground, and others explored whatever they found in the landscape, including a pile of sand for construction work. Amid all this hubbub, a tethered horse grazed, cows wandered a stone's throw away, and dogs roamed. Let's just say the place was well fertilized.

At four o'clock, we put the babies in their cribs and got on the bus to go back to our hotel, which was a good half-hour away. On the way, we stopped in Barlad, where the teaching members of our team

Play area for the children, with a clothesline, dogs, and a cow.

worked. We had all visited the school during orientation. It was a fairly typical school building with the Eastern European accoutrements of lace curtains and plenty of spider plants. The first day of school featured a welcoming ceremony for the first graders, which included a charming arch made by older students holding bouquets of flowers—crossed-sword fashion—under which the little ones passed. On the last day, students performed for our entertainment. Just like watching a parade, I found a tear in my eye when the little dancers performed the European Union anthem in hip-hop. There was also a moving rendition of "Yankee Doodle Dandy," with a verse I never knew existed. Then that evening at dinner, watching the news on TV in the hotel dining area, there was a promo for the Romanian Muscle Fantasy with oiled men in teensy briefs, shot from the biceps to the upper thighs. What an entertaining country.

Time spent away from the clinic was soaked in culture. Some of us went off for the weekend to see the painted monasteries—Biblical scenes painted on the outside (for educational purposes during illiterate times) in the 15th century. Our guide was excellent. When she explained that we were looking at a scene from heaven, and we noticed the animals in the painting, Ellen asked if that meant she would see her dog again. The answer was, "Yes." I think we were all pleased at that notion.

We also visited the university city of Iaşi, pronounced "yosh" as in "by gosh." While traveling one day, we ate lunch at McDonald's. Since I rarely eat there at home, I was unaware of their sawdust breaded chicken sandwich. Maybe it was a Romanian recipe. Also, one night we dined in a private home, where we were served homemade plum brandy. With nothing plum about it, it demanded an acquired taste, unless you were already a moonshine drinker. It arrived in small plastic bottles, like commercial water bottles, and had to be cracked open. Was this stuff made in a factory or a backyard, and if the latter, how did they get that cap sealed on there?

As we toured, we learned more and more about the country. The little trees attached to the chimneys of houses meant it was newly constructed and that the roof was done. Nuns wore little black pillbox hats with black veils over them. When the country was communist, all the nuns younger than 55 were put out on the street. Post-communism,

Painted monastery that we visited one weekend.

women were not eager to enter what might be an insecure field. In Romania at that time, priests were required to marry, but monks and nuns could not marry. At some of the monasteries, I saw quite macho looking men walking around wearing football jerseys and black skirts. Finally, I figured it out. Visitors were required to cover bare limbs, and they had entered wearing shorts. The garment also worked as a cape to cover bare shoulders.

As it was the weekend, we saw more than one family group with their cars parked at the side of the road. All the requirements for a picnic—table, chairs, food, and campfire—were installed, and everyone was dressed as if they were on their way to church. On the streets, we saw no pickup trucks but plenty of horse-drawn wagons hauling logs, lumber, hay, melons and manure. The horses sported big red tassels hanging on either side of their faces. We also ran into a young American couple who were Mennonite missionaries.

As for museums, sometimes some of the nuggets of interest are the English translations of exhibits. For instance, "Horizontal Press used at edible oil make" and "Steaza—Installation for thickening the counterpanes." As an Art History graduate student in California in the 1970s, one of my tasks was to translate titles of Chinese illustrations. I had a Chinese character dictionary and did the best I could. I imagine the results were likely the same as these.

Our other cultural learning was obtained at the hotel, which was sort of a truck stop with restaurant and bar. Younger members of the team visited the bar, but not Ellen and I. Some of us had laundry done and discovered the cost was a version of highway robbery. Then there were questions about phone charges. We hadn't made any calls and certainly not to Kabul.

Nevertheless, we felt safe there. In fact, one evening, I was in my pajamas on my bed reading—Ellen was out—and someone knocked on our door. I opened it and found a fairly agitated Romanian man holding and shaking what I thought was a cell phone. He came into the room and ranted and pointed at our television set. I gestured and indicated I didn't know what he meant. He motioned for me to come with him, so I did, even as I wondered, "Is this a good idea?" Down the hall and into his room we went, and there he pointed the object at the television and shouted, "Football, football." I shrugged and left. When I had tried to turn on our television with the remote, I had only succeeded in getting the air conditioner to blow.

We also had some language lessons. Since Romanian is from the Roman, signs were fairly readable, except for instances like the "gosh" place. A *frizerie*, for instance, is a hair salon. My journal from that trip has several pages of interesting words I had forgotten. For example, hello is *boona*, goodbye is *la revidere*—look familiar, that last one? How about *pup* (pronounced "poop") for a kiss on the cheek? Don't hit was pronounced "new lovee," and don't bite was "new moosh ka." And I found this emphatic note at the top of one page, "Don't say lemon." I'm sure after I wrote that, all I could think of was lemon, and I can't remember what it actually meant.

When we were gone on the weekends, we worried about the kids stuck in their beds all the time. One day at 4:00, our time to leave for the day, I heard Daniel shrieking from his crib and just had to go to him. I picked him up and cuddled him and then put him back down but on his stomach. He had been having respiratory problems, and that seemed to help. I told myself I couldn't think about what happens overnight or on weekends or in January and February when no volunteers came. Perhaps whatever care they received was better than what they would have had if they had stayed in their original circumstances.

I'm happy to report that when I left, Vasily's head was no longer dipping to his shoulder. One of the volunteers was an occupational therapist and had shown me some exercises for his problem. He also learned to smile and suck his thumb. His other talents included sleeping on command—it was a little like hypnotizing a chicken—and burping. I felt confident he would be able to belch the Romanian national anthem by first grade.

Our last day was tearful. I sniffed as I placed Vassily in his crib for the last time, knowing he still couldn't hold his bottle and that it would just leak onto his cheek after a while, and his rash would return. I'd done what I could for two weeks. Maybe it helped him.

Did this bit of work change me? The trip did what I had hoped it would. That is, it took me out of my world to a different culture. The work itself showed me what life is like for the innocent products of a drastically changed political system. My worldview expanded, no doubt, as I learned about circumstances outside my own powerful but beloved country. But to what end? How can my Romanian baby cuddling possibly help the less fortunate anywhere, including back home? As I remember these experiences to write about them, I realize Vasily may have prompted a decision Wally and I made to support a local

One of the toddlers living at the clinic.

women's and children's shelter. Perhaps that is the legacy of those I cared for abroad.

Or perhaps the most important part for him and for me was the cuddling and feeding, the caring for some small part of his life. He will not remember. I'll never forget. Perhaps all of life is just a sand painting, as the traveling Buddhist monks teach us. Weeks spent creating an intricate mandala with millions of grains of colored sand is simply brushed from existence when it is finished.

8

Brazil,
What's a Toy Library?—
Age 64 (2007)

I was on a roll now, traveling every year—and multiple times a year doing volunteer vacations. People had stopped asking me if I was afraid and about what my husband did while I was gone. Now they asked me where I had been recently and where I was going next. They also told me I was brave. So far, I hadn't needed bravery, so I didn't know what they meant. Brazil was the trip that gave me thoughts about fear.

In summer, I traveled to winter in the northeastern state of Bahia in Brazil, the most African part of the country. As in many Western countries, the African population began with slaves brought by those sent to colonize the area—in this case, the Portuguese. The result, after centuries, is a mixed-race place. That said, this area was communicating a pride in being nonwhite. It was evident in tee shirts for sale that said, "100% Negro." As an American who had taught in a majority-black school, and sometimes found myself the only white in a black community, I was happy to see this population. I had missed it.

I do, however, understand that crime festers in poor neighborhoods, no matter the color of the residents. That's why when our cab pulled up to the hotel where we would stay—a hotel on a dirty street with broken buildings—I thought, "Surely not here." The hotel had iron fences and gates and a guard dog, more signals for caution. On the grounds, the sense of possible harm was mitigated by the amenities of a small lawn and a swimming pool. It was indeed the place where we would stay, and we would become quite accustomed to the environment.

The hotel was small and clean and surely one of the friendliest, most comfortable places I've ever enjoyed. We ate our meals outside under an awning beside a bamboo bar. The food was brought from the kitchen, three steps away, and if we needed anything, why they just sent someone out into the street to get it. At the little bar, I would order up a *suca da manga* (fresh, sweetened mango juice) and would hear the blender whirring. There were fresh papaya and watermelon, bananas and pineapple every morning, and rich coffee, of course. There was the usual culinary oddity by American standards—chicken and corn sandwiches for breakfast one day, which weren't popular, but we did manage to go for the chocolate cake the morning it appeared.

Drums, loud, persistent drumming—that was our introduction to Pelourinho, the UNESCO world cultural center of Salvador, which was just down the street and up a hill from our hotel. Proximity to the equator evens out the daylight hours between the seasons, so it was dark soon after dinner. Every evening, we climbed what was named "shit hill" (for its distinctive fragrance) by the previous volunteers. All the streets were San Francisco-style steep and paved in particularly uneven stones. This street was actually an alley, and to make you feel safe—or to freak you out, depending on your personality—military-style guards in hard hats patrolled the streets in this part of the tourist-riddled area. They were not in that alley, however—too smelly, I think.

We were told not to wear jewelry or watches or carry purses or cameras. Forget about the value of the old or cheap watch you had decided to bring. Think about whether you want the experience of having someone take it from you because they think it is valuable. So, money and passport tucked safely near or in our undergarments or back in our room in the safes, we went forth.

These streets were the source of the drumming we heard from our hotel, just one dip in the landscape over. There are drumming teams that compete—from little kids with arms little thicker than their drumsticks to adults. Little girls danced enthusiastically in front of the kids' drumming group. The objective was to swing the hips, and when you don't have any yet, well, they were too cute in their efforts. The best group we saw was an all-woman team that slowly made their way backwards up a narrow street. Behind them was a team of men dancers—what moves. The drumbeats were at a sternum-knocking level. The drummers we saw may have been the Dida Banda Feminina, and the group behind them, Soterospolitanos, or people from Salvador who do synchronized dancing. I found them on the Internet.

The volunteer project consisted of working with sick children in a toy library in a hospital, with children and teenagers with cancer, with their mothers at a support house where they were living, and at a preschool for poor children. My friend, Ellen, and I chose the hospital work in the morning and the work at the support house in the afternoon. We were still meeting up in foreign countries to do these volunteer projects. We hadn't yet seen each other in the U.S. The toy library was a room with toys, two computers with games on them, some tables and chairs, and a hospital employee who kept very neat order. At first, I thought her constant re-shelving of the toys—in their boxes—was a little much, but after a day, I saw the logic. There was little space, and when children discarded a toy for another, it was best to keep up with the imminent chaos.

The children were all wearing little open-at-the-back hospital gowns, their undies or diapers peeking out, flip-flops on their little feet, and intravenous openings strapped to the backs of their hands. The toddlers' little hands were immobilized by being taped to a sort of board—which did not interfere in any way with playing and giggling. Parents were there with the littlest ones, and some of the older children were on their own. They all came and went for treatments or showers, whatever they needed, as they were called for by the nursing staff.

As with all my work on these trips, at some point, I questioned its usefulness. After several days of putting puzzles together, playing games, coloring, cuddling little ones and forcing my butt into a plastic chair barely large enough to hold a cantaloupe, I began my usual doubting. Then one of the fathers, who was there every day and whose little daughter was being released, came to us, shook hands and kissed us on both cheeks, Brazil style, and said through an interpreter, "God bless you, and thank you for doing this." Who knew pulling a little musical duck around and making a kid giggle could be so appreciated?

At the support houses, we arrived equipped with things to do: crocheting, knitting, drawing, jewelry making. We would set up shop,

Boys with stabilized vein sites, in their hospital gowns, playing a computer game in the toy library.

and people would come over and get involved, the mothers as interested as the children. The houses were large dormitory sorts of affairs with bunk beds and lockers, outdoor space for hanging laundry, but little in the way of hominess. They were a lot of concrete and some leftover furniture.

Many of the children were bald from chemotherapy; some were missing limbs—including little Danielle who had one leg, no hair, and the ability to have seemingly endless fun. She loved to be chased, hopping and scampering so fast you couldn't see exactly how she was doing it. No crutch in sight, she just flew. The first time I met her, she ambushed me from under a table where she was hiding. I felt a whack on my toe. I reached down with a metal knitting needle and clacked on the floor under the table to get her going, and off she went.

Ellen, a patient, her mother, and me in the toy library (courtesy Global Volunteers).

One day, a gangly teenaged girl with a large bandage enveloping her chin—and a hat to cover her baldness—was selecting a dress from some that had been donated. The women were all encouraging her to go for the slinky dressy dress, and the next day, when we arrived in the afternoon, she was wearing it, and we all made a fuss. The floppy crocheted hat, flip-flops, and bandage accessories were the same, but once again, it was all about the dress. She smiled shyly but seemed to never speak. I don't know if she could. I don't know if she ever got well.

What we did was not depressing, perhaps because we couldn't communicate verbally and discuss treatments, feelings, or prognoses. With that advantage, illness did not color the kids' identities for us. It was about hands and smiles, gestures, and understanding. Just as with the knitting, I tried to teach them about two sticks and a string. You don't really need to know any words. Perhaps our just being there was good. We were something different to look at. We spoke a different

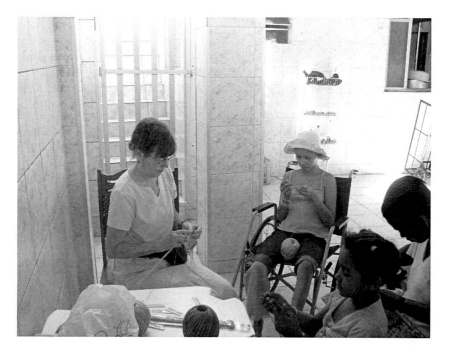

Teaching kids with cancer some yarn therapy.

language, weren't sick, and weren't treating their conditions. We were a distraction.

As for our distraction, our friendly desk clerk played the *berimbau*, an instrument resembling a large bow that's hit with a little stick and rattle. The gourd attached to one end is held against the belly and—well, suffice it to say, it has a distinctive sound and is complicated to play. One night, he escorted us to a free concert of popular music on the steps of an old church wedged between two buildings; it appeared that all three structures were condemned. He also wangled a singing gig with the feature, Gerônimo and his band, for one of our volunteers, who was a music student. The music began, and she joined in with free-form jazz singing. Gerônimo stopped playing briefly to give her one of those—wow, she's actually good—stares. The people loved her. The crowd of about a thousand was dancing in place, some drinking beer and smoking the occasional joint. A guy in dreadlocks, dark glasses and a big cushy hat carried a plastic container on his head with a spigot on the front. He was selling *cha de paz* (peace tea) according

Older boy working on a project (courtesy Global Volunteers).

to the magic marker scrawl on the side of the container. Another guy passed through the crowd with a tray of glasses with ice cubes, a can of Red Bull in the center and a bottle of scotch in his hand. Something for everyone. Little boys scavenged for discarded aluminum cans, the tabs of which were crocheted together to make clever handbags and hats sold in the market.

One evening, hasty arrangements were made for us to attend a religious service called Candomblé, a mix of African and Christian rites and beliefs. We were instructed to dress modestly in white or light-colored clothing and were rushed away in a van down one of the main streets, then off just a block or two to a modest neighborhood with brick houses. We attended a purifying ceremony in a local priest's house. Before we went in, our guide told us we needed to think about whether people actually fall into trance in the same way we approach about any religion and its articles of faith—the virgin birth, for instance, or transubstantiation, etc. We were to stand at the sides of the room, our arms at our sides.

This ceremony involved clapping but not drumming. The men and women who seemed to be the principal participants were dressed in white. The women, who were older, wore white ruffled skirts and blouses and walked about with their hands behind their backs wrapped in their skirts—and they seemed to be in a trancelike state once things got going. The priest slid his eyes up into his head to an alarming degree. At one point, young men brought out black cigars the size of cucumbers, lighted them, and gave them to the women in white, who smoked them hard and fast. At another time, the whole group said a prayer that had the cadence of the Lord's Prayer.

Then someone brought in a big heap of green branches with leaves. The women in white spent some time selecting great handfuls, until six of them ended up armed with what amounted to a couple of bushes each, one in each hand. They stood facing each other in three pairs, and then the men came forward and took turns standing between two women and being cleansed. The women passed the great, leafy bouquets over their bodies—front, back, sides, head, and feet. Then the women partook, and then we were urged to go forward and do it as well.

Ellen and I took off our shoes and stepped up. I removed my glasses and held them in my hand and closed my eyes. As they gently whacked my head, the smell of bruised leaves reminded me of happy childhood days playing in the woods, and that seemed like a blessing to me. Then we were invited to leave. The ceremony was winding down and would be followed by individual counseling sessions conducted by the priest for those seeking his advice. On the porch, we passed a sobbing woman waiting on a bench. Perhaps the counseling would help her. She and the other Brazilians attending this ceremony looked as if they had come from their day jobs in office buildings. It did not seem to be an uneducated crowd.

Everywhere in Pelourinho, we saw young, barefoot, bare-chested men in white cotton pants practicing their *capoeira* moves. *Capoeira* is a kind of martial art disguised as a dance developed by Brazilian slaves who wanted to hone their fighting skills surreptitiously. We saw teams of adult *capoeira* dancers in the squares of Pelourinho, little kids doing it in a small town we visited, and a practice session at a *capoeira* school. The finest display we saw was at the Ballet Folklorico. I wondered if this practice was the origin of break dancing.

On the weekend, we went to the beach. Ahhhh, the beach. I'm not a beach person. I grew up inland; the Atlantic seems boring, and the Pacific, too cold. Then I went to the beach in Brazil. Oh my. First, the water was cool, but not cold. The sand was fine and soft. There were no rocks to scrape my toes, and the most civilized activity of all—we sat at tables under umbrellas instead of lying in the sand. Is that a good idea or what? The tables and umbrellas were owned by a restaurant, so of course, we had to eat something. The waiter hustled over, bearing a huge tray of succulent raw seafood, all ready for us to choose from and the cook to prepare. Oysters, shrimps, a lobster all lay on a bed of greens with fruit jewels for accent. We sent him away. We weren't about to spend what that would cost. The menus were brought, and we took five stabs in the dark. However, we knew a little of what we were ordering and ended up with a delicious assortment of French fries (for the teenager), fried manioc (for me), chicken, shrimp, a little octopus salad, some rice—all of it fresh and good.

There is the problem of pests at the beach in the form of people selling things. They stroll up with jewelry and bedspreads, what looked like fried desserts, cashews measured out with a shot glass, and something grilled on a pot of coals carried around on long wires—oh, and horses, too. If you'd care to take a canter on the beach, why here's your horse, ma'am, and a pony for any little ones as well.

After our two weeks of work, Ellen and I spent our last day giving and receiving hugs and accepting construction paper valentines of thanks from the kids. It was especially meaningful to be stopped in the very street I had thought so forbidding when I arrived and to be hugged by a grateful mother.

Ellen and I had planned an extra sightseeing trip after the project. Off to Chapada Diamantina, a six-hour bus ride into the countryside, a

Girl finishing craft project above thank-you art for Ellen and me. (courtesy Global Volunteers).

trip we had arranged with a travel agent in Pelourinho. There we stayed at a little tropical sort of hotel right, I mean right, on the river. That place had the most wonderful breakfast buffet I've ever seen—tables full of fresh fruit and assorted dishes to sample. In addition, they came around with little rolls still hot from the oven, a little pancake with honey, stuff like that.

This section of Brazil is where the diamonds used to come from; people panned them from the rivers. Now such is strictly forbidden, and Brazil is trying to reclaim the land that was marred by earlier cupidity. On the first day, we dropped our bags at the hotel and followed a guide through town and off into the jungle. This land was more like a sandy forest than my movie-driven concept of jungle. We were going to some swimming places in the river. Well, no one mentioned the swimming plan, and we hadn't brought our bathing costumes, so we just took off our clothes. Ellen retained her undies, but I chucked it all, and we plunked into the water. Before we stripped, our guide had painted our faces with some colored muds he scraped from the river bottom so we could play at being Indians. What an obliging young man. Yes, a few people tromped through, but I figured I didn't know them. He also asked us if we smoked dope—the subject came up in a discussion of social problems in the small town. We said, "Not anymore." But I wondered, could we have made a connection? Does one still call it that? Would the beagles at the airport have busted us when we got back home?

On the second day, we piled into a car with two German women and a wild man at the wheel and took off for an all-day tour. The area is mountainous, and the lines of trucks were long. No worries, Brazilians interpret lines on the highway as mere suggestions. At some point, we went off-road in this rattletrap Fiat and laid down a fine yellow dust cloud past cattle and burros. Between mad dashes down dirt roads, we stopped and hiked to the top of a mesa with a view worth the whole trip, down to a cave, and up and down to a waterfall. The cave was particularly interesting as it was vast but lighted only by the gas lantern our guide carried. Four of us walked through the sandy darkness with other guides, and their people were far enough behind not to be heard. At one point, we sat on the ground, and the guide doused the light. We existed in total darkness and silence like the eyeless fish in the cave's waters. This moment turned out to be one of my soul souvenirs, as I think of it often and remember that feeling of occupying that speck on the earth, beneath the ground. I kept my eyes open in the darkness the entire time and thought this must be what blindness is like. It was not dark, nor shadowy: it was truly nothing. When I'm in trouble and need to go to a calming place in my head, I walk back into that cave and sit in the sightless silence.

On the third day, we had time only for a short hike to another river on a fairly flat trail—thank goodness. My thigh muscles were ready to revolt had my feet gone anywhere near another pile of vertical rocks. Rounding a turn on the trail, we came upon a little stand where a man sold soft drinks and candy bars, bananas and geodes and was cooking up a pot of beans in the back. It turned out that he also had diamonds. Our guide stopped to talk with the proprietor, and he mentioned that this guy still dipped up the occasional diamond from the river. We asked to see them, and he came out with rough stones and some cut ones, packaged in little sections of clear, flexible tubing with the ends stopped up. I can just imagine some of the orders he gets at his rough wood counter under the trees—gimme a beer, a plate of beans, and some carats to go. That afternoon, we boarded the bus for Salvador and our last night in Brazil, the last *suca da manga*, the last drumming lullaby.

About getting naked in public. Like my notion that you can have a different look when you are traveling, I feel that you might as well get naked if you feel like it and if it seems appropriate. Well, here's my caveat. When I stripped to dunk in the river, I hadn't thought about running into the same tourists the next day. That said, if anyone saw me as the crazy naked lady in the creek the day before with mud on her face, they didn't mention it. Besides, they were Europeans, often more relaxed about such things than Americans.

As for traveling at age 64, I had at least one indicator that my age was catching up with me. One evening going up shit hill with the other volunteers, a drunk started lurching towards us while clutching at the front of his pants. His intentions seemed, well, unfriendly, or maybe too friendly, or maybe he just had to pee. Everyone started running up that steep hill to get away from him. Ellen is almost ten years younger than I am, the next oldest was in her forties, and then there was a college student and a high school student. I felt like the old one left behind by the herd when the lion caught a whiff of us. All I saw were the bottoms of their sandals, pumping elbows, and the seats of their pants as they took off. The guy was too wasted to do any harm, so he never touched us, but we sent one of the gentlemen dressed in military garb and a helmet down to have a word with him, nevertheless.

Fear is an interesting state of mind. The fears I vanquished back in Virginia when I stayed alone in the country were certainly generated by my own mind. The leery feeling I had when we saw the neighborhood where we would stay on this trip was an assessment. That's a good thing to have in a new situation. Knowing the difference helps a great deal.

9

Armenia,
Apricots and Rubble—
Age 65 (2008)

By 2008, I had been retired for a while, so it was easy to find the time to take multiple trips a year. This was the first year I made three trips abroad. I was picking up momentum. After a tour of Morocco, my next adventure was a volunteer trip, unlike any of my previous volunteer trips or my other trips made just as a tourist. It was with Earthwatch in Armenia. We worked with a professor of architecture on her research, which aimed to document and possibly promote the vernacular residential architecture of the Kumayri Historic District in Gyumri, Armenia. The measurements we made and the drawings we did of the houses in Gyumri are the actual data upon which her research was based. The work was going to be more technical than I had done on other volunteer trips.

At that time, Earthwatch required a doctor to sign off on your ability to perform the kinds of tasks they describe for each project. This one wasn't strenuous, so I wasn't worried. Their briefing was quite thorough and included potential hazards from vehicles that might not have seat belts to the fact that Armenia is in an earthquake zone. Also, there was a nuclear reactor on the eastern Anatolia fault line, 31 miles from where we would be working. Add to that, dangers from stray dogs, allergic reactions to plants, etc. Kaye, my friend who had lived in Armenia for several years, had already warned me about the condition of the hospitals when she related how she was taken in what seemed like a Korean War-era MASH ambulance to a hospital after she fell in her home in Yerevan. At age 65, I was still feeling pretty frisky and didn't worry about any of that.

9. *Armenia, Apricots and Rubble*

This trip seemed rich in a different way than others because of the connections I was able to make thanks to Kaye. She arranged for a couple of personal tours by her old friends who still lived in Armenia. Through Kaye's introductions, Ellen, my traveling companion on this trip, and I met and were entertained by an American and an Armenian on two separate occasions while in the capital, Yerevan, a city that got its start as a fortress in 782 BCE.

Before this trip, all I knew about Armenia was that during my childhood, Armenian children had been starving. I was reminded of this any time I didn't finish my supper. The logic always failed me since my uneaten food wasn't being shipped off to help those kids, and it would never get there in edible condition if it were.

Our first sight of Armenia from the plane included Mount Ararat in all its snowy glory. The mountain is actually in Turkey now, but it is beloved and esteemed by Armenians. It appears in their art, their décor, and their kitchen windows. The story goes that after Noah and the animals landed on Mt. Ararat, his descendants, Hayk and Armen, eventually led their tribe out of Babylon into eastern Anatolia and settled at the foot of Mt. Ararat. Over time, the tribe grew and became a sovereign state known as Hayastan, the name currently used by Armenians when referring to their homeland. That mountain's presence cannot be ignored, in the landscape or in the hearts of the Armenians. They would, in fact, like very much to have it back.

Passengers being greeted by friends and relatives at the airport carried bouquets of fresh flowers in brilliant colors; Armenians love to give flowers. And the women carrying them were dressed like they were going to a fancy party—all strappy high heels, sheer dresses, and glitzy bags. Never mind that the streets are mere suggestions of pavement and that many of their men are gone to Russia to work. There was no slacking in the fashion department.

Ellen and I arrived a day early, and Kaye's friend, Mary, came by our hotel the first thing the next morning and took us all over the city on foot from right after breakfast until dinner time. It was wonderful to have an American telling us all about the sights we saw—from the cascades, a huge construction of stairs, sculpture and fountains, to the Vernissage, the weekend outdoor market. There you can buy everything from plumbing parts and handmade carpets to jewelry and old

Soviet medals. When we were walked out, she took us to her apartment, served us homemade cookies and lemonade, and then showed us her incredible quilted work. When we got back to our hotel, we joined the others in our group and went to a Georgian restaurant for a really nice dinner of little headache-ice bag-shaped dumplings filled with juice and meat. That night I discovered that all the walking and the heat of the day had added up to blistered feet for me.

When the guidebook I bought included, as a separate country, a place called Nagorno-Karabakh (which I had never heard of), I knew I was going to learn a lot. Nagorno-Karabakh was described as "an Armenian separatist enclave in Azerbaijan" in the *New York Times* in April 2016, when an ethnic flare-up between that country and Armenia was reported. All was quiet when I was there.

In addition to all Armenia's political upheavals through the years, it has been divided and passed around between Iran, Turkey and the Soviet Union. In 1988, Armenia was hit with a powerful earthquake.

Hare on a Bell by Barry Flanagan at the Cascade in Yerevan (courtesy Ellen Westbrook).

9. Armenia, Apricots and Rubble

Twenty years later, people were still living in *domics*, which are metal shipping containers, and also in the old houses that were in need of major repair. Imagine a tree growing in the ruined second floor of your house, which is what we found in one home. Where we worked, the country was hit with a triple whammy about the same time: the earthquake

Lace work for sale at the Vernissage in Yerevan (courtesy Ellen Westbrook).

in 1988, a war with Azerbaijan, and then the collapse of the Soviet Union in 1991.

The next day we were off to Gyumri in a van with our luggage stuffed in beside us. We stopped several times to get out and take photographs of the raging wildflowers blanketing the fields, while in the distance, the folds of the hills were still white with snow. In Gyumri, we settled into our room at the Hotel Berlin (built by the German Red Cross), a quiet place with rooms and a garden filled with art by local artists. It's the kind of place where you can wear your slippers to breakfast and in the evening might hear the desk clerk playing the piano for a little while just because he felt like it. One morning, the women who worked there were playing music and began dancing, and some of us joined them before heading out to work. It was a pleasant place to call home for two weeks.

The confused economy was evident everywhere, from the abandoned factories with haunting broken windows to the Hummers parked next to piles of rubble outside damaged houses. In Gyumri, the

New buildings going up next to rubble.

streets were dust and holes with a little pavement sprinkled here and there. Building cranes were everywhere, as new glass box-like buildings went up beside the rubble.

In the morning, we had a long lecture about how to measure spaces and draw accurate elevations and floor plans, one made arduous by fatigue and remaining jet lag. I had been ready to suggest they call in the bulldozers and wondered why they wanted to save this stuff, to begin with. My ugly American, who had never accompanied me on a trip before, was struggling to surface, but I didn't let her out. This was going to be hard work, and the hours would be long. We practiced by measuring rooms in the hotel, and then we went to an actual house and worked in the afternoon until seven that night. The lady of the house served us coffee, pastries, fresh apricots, juice and candy, all on fine china. Our little group was under the impression we had to measure the whole house (kitchen, living room, porch) in one afternoon. Turned out that we had the whole time we would be there. That put a different spin on it. What a relief—no more thoughts of demolition. At

Renovated house next to attached house needing renovation.

9:30 that night, Ellen and I finally found the closest Internet café and joined the local nerds to communicate with those back home.

On the way back from lunch one day, we toured an interesting children's aesthetics school that was filled with art created by the students. It was nice to see art promoted in children's education. My experience back home was of slashed art budgets in schools, and when there was an art program, well, it too often involved learning to make the right kind of Easter bunny out of colored paper. This was freewheeling expression. These children painted pink-and-yellow chickens with orange wings and purple tail feathers—happy chickens. Another had a turtle strolling through wildflowers beneath a purple sky filled with toothy clouds.

On a less colorful note, we had been told about the people mentioned above, who were still living 20 years later in containers because of the 1988 earthquake. At lunch one day, I was sitting there wondering out loud what it must be like for any people who had been born right around the time of the earthquake and grew up in a container, when the young man next to me, one of our helper/interpreters, told me he

Children's cheerful painting.

lived in one with his mother and always had. He was a few months old when the earthquake struck. He happened to have a scholarship to a university in Utah and had lived in the U.S. one school term. He was working on this project while home for the summer. I could not imagine the cultural swerve he took from living in a *domic* to flying to the U.S. and attending a university there. The *domics*, rectangular metal shipping containers had windows and doors in them and wood stoves for heat. No water or electricity was provided. People made changes to them through the years by adding windows, patching the roof, laying a wood floor, maybe. They were rusting industrial versions of shanties.

There comes the day on any trip when things don't go too well. Here's a synopsis of one. Prepare for a fine whine. The owner of the house we were working on wouldn't let us in to work in the afternoon. However, her neighbor befriended us, brought us into her kitchen, and gave us something to drink. It was a watery yogurt drink with dill in it, which was good but not in the amount she gave me, and the blisters on my foot were really painful, and things were getting frustrating because we really couldn't get our work done and so there was a change of plan. Can you hear the whining? I limped over to a museum with the group and looked at two big art exhibits. One was interesting, but the other one was by some sculptor who apparently specialized in death masks of Russians. By then, my sense of humor had really run out, and I thought, "Great, a big room filled with dead heads."

I really needed a break, so I decided, in the gloom of my own mind, that I wouldn't be going on the excursion planned for 6:30. I limped, grim-faced, back to the hotel, where I put my feet up and had an antacid—and some chocolate, just to make sure. I was resting comfortably when there was a knock on the door from the translator. Sorry for the interruption. Did I mind? We were going to be interviewed for a television program. Our architect boss did all the talking, and we nodded. Then the excursion got changed to the next day for some reason, and we went to dinner. But before dinner, I used my oil pastels to do some painting and got all happy again. Just a brief sinking spell. The trick is to shut up until the mood passes.

One evening, things got really interesting after I left the Internet café. It was almost dark, but people were out with their kids; it was not a scary part of town or anything. I was limping along, and this

The author at the door to the courtyard and building where she started work each morning (courtesy Ellen Westbrook).

man walked up beside me from behind and asked, in English, if I was all right. I said I was. He told me he couldn't speak English, in English, and wiggled the tip of his tongue at me in a way that suggested, well, you know what it suggests. Then he would ask me again if I was all right, with a sort of concerned look, then that tongue would snake

Entrance to our work place, with a small door cut into the larger door for easy entry.

out again. He was just some ordinary-looking guy, and I thought, "Did he really do that thing with his tongue?" He did it again, and when I turned in at the gate to the hotel, he came along and kept calling stuff out to me and caught up again and said he liked me and wanted...

I kept saying, "No, no, no, no," and heading for the door, limpety-limp, as fast as I could. The man didn't come into the lobby. If he had, I knew the piano playing desk clerk would take care of business. I kept thinking, do hookers stay at the hotel? How could I be mistaken for a hooker in my old lady stretchy waist pants, white socks, and sandals when the ordinary women wear sequins, short sheer skirts, and heels so spiked they could skewer ants. He was younger than I, so then I figured it was someone with a mother complex. When I told Ellen what happened, she said she didn't know whether to sympathize with me or congratulate me. I said that at my age, I preferred the latter. Besides, there were lots of people around, so I wasn't really scared, more like astonished.

The delayed excursion was to the Red Fort. It is huge and round and closed up, but we got to walk around it and hear about it. There were groups of Armenians frolicking about, picking wildflowers and having their pictures taken—by them, by us and with us, at their request. Somewhere in Armenia, there are pictures of me grinning away in my stupid, foldable sun hat. Then we went down the road a piece and looked at the Soviet-built *Mother Armenia* statue. She is so large that, looking up from her feet, one breast appeared to be the size of a Buick parked perilously off the side of a bridge. She holds a sheaf of wheat aloft in one hand and in the other, what looks like a flowerpot with a sandwich on top. So much for monumental Soviet art.

About food there, the Armenians served everything in really small dishes, sort of an individual salad plate size, but you'd be surprised: you pass it around, and everyone takes a little, and there's still enough for seconds. One night, we had something called cat's whiskers. It's a little meatloaf kind of thing wrapped around uncooked pasta, so the ends stick out like whiskers. I think they steam it. One day we had *lahmajoo*n (pronounced, llama John), a thin, round Armenian pizza kind of dish. The stuff we had previously, which I had thought was Armenian pizza, was just pizza made in Armenia. This *lahmajoon* stuff was served with bottles of liquid yogurt or kefir, not sure which. I had a beer.

We woke to bad news—a wall of stone in some new construction fell on a *domic* and killed three people inside. They were supposed to clear out all the dwellings next to the construction for safety's sake, but they hadn't. The *domic* was right beside a three-story wall in a block we were surveying from the outside. We stayed away for a day out of respect for the people who were gathering at a nearby house to mourn and console each other.

One day we quit work around 5:30 and went to see a carpet-making

A typical electrical tangle waiting for disaster.

demonstration. A woman was seated on the floor, working like lightning on a small vertical loom in her kitchen. She worked all day in a carpet factory and worked again at home to supplement her income, which she said was too small. Her daughter was going to university, and she needed money. Some of us went back the next night and bought

Armenian woman weaving in her home after work. I own that small rug now.

the small pieces she had been weaving. I am so glad I have that piece. I have always had a special appreciation for handwork and the way it manifests our time on earth. The carpet is small, just 20 by 25 inches, but all those stitches came together to make a beautiful textile. The price was 12,000 dram or about $34. I hope it helped with her daughter's education.

We got Saturday off and went on a trip through the countryside to see some very old churches, the very large Lake Sevan, and some beautiful forests. Our first stop was at a place where people dined in little log structures beside the river. Some of them were balconied out over the water. The walkways were lined with blooming roses, and there were numerous and differently-sized little buildings with tables and chairs in them, sort of playhouses for adults. The kitchen was outdoors, and waiters brought our coffee and snacks to our little house. Everything was light and airy inside because of all the windows, the white tablecloth, and the lace curtains. As we left, I saw a live sheep tied up and lying on its side in front of the kitchen—someone's dinner waiting to happen. A large dog lay nearby, keeping it company. People sometimes slaughtered sheep or goats to honor a member of the family.

At one of the church sites, we saw some very old *khatchkars*, or stone crosses, and near them some small trees decorated with handkerchiefs and rags tied to the branches, making wishes. We were told it is a custom left from pagan times. While sitting on a bench near the Goshavank monastery complex, built in the late 12th century, I saw a man get off a bus and unload the two-by-fours he brought home through the bus window. I'm guessing he would wish for a pickup truck when he tied a rag to a tree.

I learned to make coffee one night in a *gazva* (pronounced "jazz-vah"). It's just a little open pot with a handle and pouring lip. I learned this in the hotel kitchen, which is just a little room off the reception area. One of the women who worked at the hotel took me in and showed me how to measure cups of water into the pot, then add heaping spoons of coffee so finely ground it is like powder, a little spoonful of sugar, and put it on the heat. Take it off when it comes to a boil, stir, and pour.

At every meal, we had the traditional bread called *lavash*. It is very thin—a sort of tissue paper made of bread. From a sheet of it, you tear off a piece, wrap food in it, and eat it. The amazing thing is how it's made. The house we were measuring had a *lavash* bakery in the back of it, so we got to see the process first-hand. The dough is formed into balls and then rolled out into long oval sheets about two feet long. Then a thin sheet of dough is flopped onto a large, heavy canvas pillow mounted on a board with a handle on the back. Then a person whacks the dough into place against the inside of a vertical, cylindrical oven (called a *tonir*) that is flaming up at him. The pillow thing is then removed. The dough sticks to the oven wall and is then peeled off shortly thereafter. It's hot work, and the person who does it wears long sleeves and maybe gloves. The story is that *lavash* keeps for weeks or months. Just sprinkle a little water on it to refresh it.

There was a delegation at the hotel one day. All the men gathered around the tables, near the lobby, where we ate, and the few women in the group were in the small lounge area near our room. The men were standing up, then sitting down, saying things, then doing it all again. They were toasting each other and who knows what else with vodka and cognac. It was 8:30 in the morning.

Life at the Internet café was always a hoot. There was a gaming session one day, and the place was filled—all six computers. Another night, there were only four of us in there, Ellen, the proprietor, some other guy, and me. They were apparently yanking some guy's chain on Skype. Another day while I was there, they sent out for beer. After the beer, they set up a small electric plate to make coffee in a *gazva*; they then sipped the coffee from china demitasse cups and saucers they had pulled out of a desk drawer. Nerds in their macho leather jackets, sipping from the little cups their grandmothers probably gave them.

On our last day, we delivered presents to the family whose house we measured, and the gifts were a big hit: books for the children and framed photos of the kids for their mother, pictures we had during our work. Then we went around and gave prints to the neighbors whom we'd photographed. They were all beside themselves and competing to bring us into their houses for coffee. We stayed with our hostess and had coffee, cookies, candies and apricots. I ate fifty times more apricots while I was in Armenia than I'd eaten in my life until then, and every one of them was perfect. The trees and markets were full of them. People were often seen seated next to piles of them, elbows on knees, peelings and pits dropping into a bucket between their feet. Just imagining the jam they would make was mouthwatering.

We had dinner at the fish farm. I was thinking that I'm probably not going to like this because I am not fond of freshwater fish. We went by cab, and the streets were so bad we had to go in slow, sharp zigzags to avoid the holes in the road. Then we passed right next to a Russian army base, and I thought. "Hmmm, the fish are raised downstream from this place." My attitude was less than enthusiastic, but then we walked down really pretty stone stairs to the bottom of a canyon and came to the fish farm. The water is particularly cold there, and they are able to raise four kinds of trout, plus Siberian sturgeon. Supposedly the oxygen-rich alkaline water produces a superior fish. The preliminary dishes included fish liver and fish eggs. I tried both. Then we had sturgeon, which was lowered into a *tonir* in a rack. It was the best fish I have ever eaten. By the way, they chilled the red wine and not the white wine, as if we cared.

When our work was completed and we were on our way back to Yerevan, we stopped at the Armenian Genocide memorial and spent some time there. According to the Armenian National Institute, in April 1915, the Ottoman government began to systematically decimate the civilian Armenian population. The persecutions continued until 1923 when the Ottoman Empire ceased to exist and was replaced by the Republic of Turkey. The Armenian population of the Ottoman state was reported at about two million in 1915. An estimated one million had perished by 1918, while hundreds of thousands had become homeless and stateless refugees. By 1923, virtually the entire Armenian population of Anatolian Turkey had disappeared. As I learned more about this history, I realized the source of the suppertime comments about the Armenian children when I was young. Turkey still disputes the event as being a genocide.

Nevertheless, the memorial is impressive architecturally and has a splendid view of Mt. Ararat, which seems to float in the sky in the distance above Turkey, the country that prompted the place. The eternal flame, monolith, walkways and museum are all serene and calm in design, and the mood is enhanced by ever-present but unobtrusive *a cappella* opera music. The photographs in the museum, however, can be quite disturbing—men sitting at tables with severed heads in front of them facing the camera. I made short work of my time in there and went out to enjoy the gardens and memorial. I reviewed my convictions that we humans are capable of the worst evil and my belief that our capacity for good exceeds that ability. I tell myself that if it did not, we would not exist, and the insects and birds would fill our once noisy, voice-filled places with their music.

An example of that very goodness was the owner of the B&B, where Ellen and I stayed in Yerevan. He was an Italian physician who talked with us about the work he'd been doing in Armenia since the earthquake. He's from Sicily and came to help the victims and had been working to help restore the country since then. Proceeds from the B&B went to support a hospital for mothers and children, and there was also a school that trained people in making ceramics. It was a pleasure to meet someone who had set out to help people and was successfully doing it.

Ellen and I booked a post-project tour of the ancient temple at Garni and the monastery at Geghard, which is built right into the rock. It's a day trip from Yerevan. After booking, we wandered around the city and had lunch at an outdoor cafe. As the menu was only in Armenian, I asked what the lady was having at the next table and was told it was a hot dog, so I ordered a hot dog and a beer. The wiener came split lengthwise on a small loaf of bread and had tomatoes, cucumbers and mayonnaise on it. While we were sitting there, a man came along with a rough sack of raw hazelnuts. He stopped and solemnly gave each of us one nut and then went on his way without a word.

Our excursion was in a minivan with three young women, the guide, and the driver to the Greco-Roman temple at Garni and then on to the monastery at Geghard. Very interesting, but I often find the surroundings more interesting than the historical places. At this one, there were people selling stuff outside, and Ellen and I bought something called sweet bread and something else that looked like a raw sausage, but it was actually made of fruit and nuts. It was called *shugugh*. We gobbled it. There were also animal pelts of fox and wolf, intriguing but hardly transportable, with U.S. Fish and Wildlife Service doggies sniffing luggage at the airports.

After dinner one night, we went to the movies. What did it matter that *Indiana Jones and the Crystal Skull* was in Russian without subtitles? We could follow that kind of plot. We got our tickets and went upstairs in this huge building and were told by a woman with a badge (Armenian power *pani*) that we couldn't go in yet. At the instant the movie was over, the people came out, and we went in. It was a big theater with nice, cushy seats, but only about thirty or so people were attending. At the stroke of seven or as soon as we all sat down, the movie began. And when it was over, they shut it off. Never mind if you wanted to read the credits at the end. Time to go home. Get out.

At the beginning of our trip and the first time through Yerevan, we had met an American artist. We reconnected with her, and she took us to visit an English-speaking Armenian artist at her apartment, where she had prepared a large lunch for us, including a meat dish. She was a vegetarian. She gave me a small painting, and I also bought one from her before we left. It was a pleasant visit and nice to see inside a typical Soviet-built concrete apartment again. Armenian carpets helped soften the interiors.

We also met a young Armenian woman Kaye had told me about. Zara worked as an interpreter. We asked if she could go with us to the Vernisage again so she could help us buy things. I had admired the artwork at the hotel, which contained figures from Armenian caves. Zara spoke to a bookseller, who had just the book I needed. Once home, these figures began to appear in my artwork, and still do.

Back at the hotel, our cab driver tried to tell us we owed 2,000 drams. Six hundred had been the usual, and that was high, but we argued and offered what we thought it was worth—there was laughing, etc., but he didn't want what we were trying to give him and said the fare was nothing. So I gave him nothing and heard grumbling about petrol prices, etc., as I got out and slammed the door. Oh, well, the hotel was providing a driver to get us to the airport at 6:00 the next morning, so we wouldn't be running into him again. At the airport, we gave Armenia our last 10,000 drams in exit fees and then headed for home.

I was now convinced I didn't need to do any more volunteer teaching. I also learned that I had to take care of my feet: heat and pavement were a bad combination for me. That meant choosing places that did not include cities in hot weather. My travel destinations and activities would now be more carefully planned.

119

10

South Africa, Following Meerkats— Age 67 (2010)

The change from volunteer teaching to more active projects was suiting me, and if I was going to go to the Kalahari and see meerkats up close, it was time to do it. Meerkats: you know, those cute, fuzzy little animals that stand on their hind legs in a row and seem to worship the sun. You've seen them in *National Geographic* and on television. Well, I was off on another Earthwatch expedition, this time to South Africa to work with the scientists who study them. It was my first wildlife adventure and my first time totally out of touch with Wally.

Crossing the Atlantic and part of Africa took more than 16 hours. As we approached Johannesburg, I saw strange mounds in the brown earth and what appeared to be ponds beside them. They were mines. South Africa is the land of gold and diamonds.

Because I entered the country in Johannesburg, I had to collect my luggage and go through customs. Both pieces, my small suitcase and a backpack filled with things for a school we would visit, arrived safely. The backpack had come undone, and socks were spilling out, but nothing was lost. South Africa had been hosting the World Cup in soccer, and immigration was all set up to handle the crowds, so I passed through quickly and then caught another plane to head back west to my destination, Cape Town. I arrived at night to see the city like a spangled jewel in the clear night air. The Atlantic Ocean made a dark background for the edge of the display below.

After landing and collecting my bags again, I headed for the exit and looked for someone holding a sign with my name on it, as I had arranged for the hotel to send someone to get me. I saw names, but not mine. Then I spotted a man hurriedly approaching and reaching inside his coat for a sheet of paper. He held it up, and there it was, "Jody Shwab"—close enough.

Archie turned out to be a very personable man who carried my bags and began my sightseeing tour that very night. I was his only passenger, and when he suggested that I crawl up between the seats in the van and sit next to him, like he was my uncle or something, I did.

Archie pointed out the huge area of shacks (called a township) where the black people lived. He said he was a coloured (local spelling) man (meaning mixed-race) and would be in danger going to the projects alone after dark. The townships were the homes of tribal people with purely Negro blood. Later I would get to see more of these areas.

Let me say this about racial terminology. Outside the U.S., people use different vocabularies for ethnic groups. Some of these names fall outside the U.S. parameters for political correctness. When I was growing up in the fifties, my parents carefully instructed me in the polite term for referring to the people we call African Americans today. It was *colored,* not *Negro,* and certainly not the other "N" word. Archie looked like the people we call black in America. To me, black Africans do not look like our black neighbors and friends back home. It's a different country with different terminology and different race issues, like the issue in Bahia in Brazil.

We passed the hospital where Dr. Christiaan Barnard performed the first heart transplant and then came to the downtown area where I would be staying. It was full of merrymakers blowing *vuvuzelas,* extremely loud horns, celebrating soccer game goals. Our hotel, the Grand Daddy, had a penthouse on the roof consisting of individual Airstream trailers, each with its own rural mailbox on a post, a little picket fence, and a fake lawn. There was a bar on the roof as well as a large sitting area with leather sofas, tables, and a huge television screen.

Archie dropped me off, and the guys carrying my bags took me to the roof and knocked on the door of one of the Airstreams. Ellen, my old traveling friend, greeted me with a big smile and hug. She was in her pajamas and reported that the tiny bathroom had lots of very hot water. Our trailer was named "Pleasantville" and was decorated in an American fifties theme. Ellen and I caught up, and I tried to get my jet-lagged brain and body to work—then a shower and into a very comfortable bed.

We woke to rain but bundled up and went downstairs to the restaurant for our included breakfast, a sort of full English breakfast with a healthy twist—yogurt instead of baked beans. Then we shopped up and down the street. Ellen had already been through the area and said she didn't mind doing everything again. We bought hand-beaded necklaces, key fobs made from soda-can metal, and eland fur pillows, and ran into Archie at the supermarket. I bought an umbrella, and it worked like a charm—stopped raining for the rest of the trip.

After that, we went to the Victoria and Alfred waterfront, which is filled with shops and restaurants. We went to the aquarium there and enjoyed that, too. More shopping, then a movie, then dinner in a sports bar—more World Cup. While there, our waiter asked us where we were from, and we told him the U.S. He said he was also a foreigner in South Africa. He was Angolan. I realized his saying he was a foreigner struck me as odd for a nanosecond. Then I realized, on this first trip to sub-Saharan Africa, I was confusing a country with a continent. Of course, he was a foreigner.

The Angolan went on to tell us about how the South Africans kill the black foreigners who come there. He said he had friends who had been murdered and that as soon as the World Cup was over, it would start up again. Now there was a sobering note. We pondered it on the way back to the hotel. It wasn't until I was doing some research for this book that I discovered how high the murder rate was in South Africa in 2010. Much of what I read indicated crime was most likely in the townships and even more likely in Johannesburg. Lack of work and money were cited as causes for frustration high enough to take lives. What the waiter told us seemed likely to be true. The research also brought home the alarming murder rate in the U.S. compared with other parts of the world—something not easy to register back home where I live in a fairly safe environment.

No rain and sunny the next day, and people were still blowing the *vuvuzelas*. Apparently, the spectators at the World Cup games blow them constantly. On the television at the restaurant, it sounded like a huge hive. From our rooftop, they sounded like wild animals calling to each other in agony. We had arranged, through the hotel, to get Archie to take us on a half-day tour. Getting out of the city, I saw how amazing the southern cape of Africa is. The sky went on forever, and the mountains in the distance were sharpened by the clear air. We passed fields with healthy-looking Herefords grazing alongside ostriches and springbok.

First, we stopped at a tourist place where they had cheetahs on which they were doing DNA research. Some event about 12,000 years ago wiped out all but a few cheetahs, and they then interbred. This inbreeding has resulted in all cheetahs being so closely related that they are vulnerable to the same diseases and are at great risk for extinction. These cats were born in captivity and then moved to this place. We watched the people who work there play with them. If you paid a little fee, you could go inside and pet one and have your picture taken with an animal. It somehow seemed disrespectful to the animal, so I didn't do it.

Our lunch was in a treehouse. There were a bunch of them spaced fairly far apart. Each had a system of crude copper piping and various forms of fountains below. Water ran through the pipes and off the ends and down underneath, very charming. We went up winding steps to our table and ordered drinks. Then a woman came up with a pitcher, basin, and towel and poured warm water over our hands as we held them over the basin in her other hand. Then we dried them on the towel. She went away and then came back and painted pretty white designs on our faces. I noticed the white looked better on the guests whose skin provided a contrast than on our pale skin.

After that, we were brought salad and breads, dips and herbs. When we had eaten that, we went downstairs to a huge buffet in a tent and loaded up on lamb, gemsbok, chicken, fish, fruit, vegetables, including pumpkin, and sauces. Then we went up, polished that off, and went back down for dessert. At one point during our meal, it began to rain just a little. The waiter rushed up and moved a leaf-shaped piece of sheet metal, the size of a dining room table, from the side and over our heads, and we were cozy as could be.

Archie said he would throw in a drive through a township. Ellen had not been interested in touring a township. She said she didn't mind driving through, but she didn't want to go into anyone's home. I agreed.

Archie told us that the blacks and the coloreds don't mix, and that the blacks from different tribes don't mix. In fact, the township we went through was made up entirely of people from the Zulu tribe. We told Archie what the waiter had told us, and Archie's view was that the foreigners bring in drugs and take housing that was meant for South Africans—another side of it.

Archie explained that the whole township began when men came to the area to work from farther north on the cape and lived in government-provided hostels. When their families joined them, they all crowded into the little rooms. Now the township is acres of shacks made of scrap lumber and rusted, corrugated steel, cheek by jowl. Sometimes you see a line of privies that seems to go on forever, not a finger's width between them.

These neighborhoods take up what must be acres of space. The houses are tiny and lean this way and that. The paths and streets have litter, old tires, cardboard, and rubble. Leaking roofs are covered with flapping tarps weighted with rocks. Cars are in wretched shape and sometimes have no lights or brakes. Among it all, flapping laundry dries. These are home to thousands of people.

Back at the hotel, a different world altogether, we watched the last game of the World Cup on the big screen right there on the roof with a bunch of other people—and had free drinks. We wrapped up in the wool blankets on the leather sofas provided by the hotel and rooted for a team chosen at random. Thank goodness no one was blowing a *vuvuzela.*

The next day we went to Table Mountain on the cable car. I thought it was going to be all about the view from up there, but although that was stunning, the walk along the top of the mountain was a gift for the senses after the city. Up there, there are animals called dassies (hyraxes) that look a lot like groundhogs and are, oddly enough, the closest relative of the elephant—something easier to comprehend when you realize elephants used to be the size of rabbits. Ellen and I walked around, and I just sucked in the color of the rocks and the flowering shrubs and the pools of rainwater in the rock. Then we had tea and rusks in the little café. Rusks are small, very, very, very stale cakes. If you don't have something to dunk it in, just put it aside for packing material. Then back down on the cable car, which rotated as it traveled.

124

Cape Town may be the most beautiful city I've ever visited. We caught a cab and went to the Company Gardens, then shopped, dined, and found an Internet café, from which I sent what would be my last message to Wally for two weeks—a long time for us, a couple of introverts married 44 years at that time.

As I was checking in at the airport the next morning, a man said Upington—my destination—was having a cold spell. That made me think I had probably brought the right clothes. I was so wrong.

Upington turned out to be a town of about 20,000. The plane landed, and we collected our luggage and headed for the exit. Someone called my name, and we turned to meet Melissa, the project manager. She loaded all six of us into a van-like vehicle that was towing a trailer with a tarp over it. We packed our luggage into the trailer, piled into the vehicle, and headed downtown. Melissa dropped us off at a sort of strip mall, where we could buy the things we thought we might want in the next two weeks, items that were not included in the program. We had a supermarket for snacks, a café for lunch, and a computer Internet café, which was just a film store with one computer they let you use. I decided to be dry in the desert and didn't go to the liquor store. In Upington everyone seemed to be speaking Afrikaans, switching to English when they realized you didn't understand them.

After lunch, Melissa came to collect us. I took the seat up front and got to ask her questions. The trip is three hours long over a rough dirt road, and she drove as if it were a race. Melissa is a native. Her first language is Afrikaans, and her second, English. South Africans study English in school and must also study a native language. The country has 11 official languages: Afrikaans, English, IsiNdebele, IsiXhosa, IsiZulu, Sepedi, Sesotho, Setswana, SiSwati, Tshivenda, and Xitsonga.

A young, attractive woman, Melissa was planning to marry a local farmer soon. He had a small farm of more than 3,000 hectares. That's nearly 7,500 acres of game farm. Springbok, gemsbok, and elands— all the animals we only see in a zoo at home—are roving around these great farms and are eaten. I asked her how they rounded them up, and she said with a *bakkie* (truck) or with motorcycles. Because of the country's strict gun laws, they hire a farmer with a license to own guns to come in and shoot the animals when they need to do that.

We arrived at the Kuruman River Reserve and got out into the dusty Kalahari. When the tarp was pulled back from our cargo in the trailer (our luggage and the week's groceries), everything was coated with an inch of sifted road dust, finer than flour.

Our first stop was at the farmhouse, where most of the researchers lived. Melissa handed out boxes of food and individual packages of beer, wine, and liquor that she had brought them at their request. Then we got back in and got ourselves over to where we were going to stay and unloaded. It was dark, but we could see the round huts called *rondavels*, with their conical thatched roofs, where we would live. Melissa

Road dust on my suitcase in the doorway of my *rondavel*. I had already whacked the top layer of dust off.

gave us our keys, and we hauled our filthy luggage through the sand to our individual little homes.

Inside I found two windows with drapes, a single bed, a small folding table for a desk, a desk lamp, an electric kettle, a bureau, a footlocker with a padlock, a small cold-water sink, and a tiny heater. But most importantly, there was a hot water bottle on the bed. The place was freezing cold. It took a while to figure out how to turn on the heater. At dinner (curried lamb, rice and *dahl*), we were joined by two men, the manager and another who had recently written an article for the *London Times* about the meerkat project. I was not picking up much verbally as everyone had a British accent, and there was a lot of resonance in the building. Needed to see about those hearing aids when I got home.

The bathrooms were in an unheated masonry building. The toilet seats were so cold I forgot what I sat down to do. The tap water was scalding, and I filled my hot water bottle, put on my flannel nightgown, pajama bottoms, socks, a scarf around my neck, wool mitts on my hands, and a wool sweater with the hood over my head and got into bed. Thank goodness the bed was covered with a double-thick wool blanket, a fleece blanket, and a duvet. I turned on my headlamp and read a little before trying to get to sleep. Had to be up at 6:00 a.m.

Up on time, in the dark, I looked in the mirror and saw a grumpy old woman with her hair standing straight out from her head because of the dry air. I plugged in my kettle, got dressed, including all jackets, and headed for the bathroom. When I came back, the power for the heater was out. Only the puny overhead lamp worked. As it turned out, everyone had this problem. It was 28° F. The main house where we ate was also cold, so there was no place to get warm.

Breakfast meant going into the kitchen and making something (same for lunch). I had coffee someone else had made, yogurt and muesli because it was easy. Then we loaded into one of the vehicles and went through gates to the farmhouse. A beautiful racing pigeon strutted about the front yard. He flew in one day and decided to stay. They named him Mick Jagger and didn't like it when he went into the kitchen.

The living room of the farmhouse was full of old, overstuffed furniture that any self-respecting redneck would refuse to put on the porch for the dogs. The researchers were getting ready to go out for the morning's work. Each of us would be paired up with one of them. They were all bundled to the eyes in an assortment of clothing; whatever was warm, they piled on. These men and women were stuffing big backpacks with equipment and gear. They had radios and GPS gadgets hanging off their pants, and VHF antennas bristled from their packs.

Ellen and I were assigned to go to the Whiskers group. These meerkats are famous as they were the stars in the *Meerkat Manor* television series, which I knew of but had not seen. I was wearing jeans, socks with hiking boots, a shirt, a wool sweater, a silk scarf, a wool hat, a fleece jacket with a wind-breaking parka over it, and light gloves. Soon I pulled my sweater hood up under my hat and added wool mitts to my hands. While waiting for the meerkats to come out of their burrows, I shivered and mentally went through my luggage to figure out what I could add to my costume the next day. I decided on everything.

Finally, the meerkats begin to emerge and stand in the sun, just the way we were, and for the same reason—to get warm. We were instructed to hum three notes around them every now and then, as researchers had used this formula while habituating them. We were standing there shivering and hmmm, hmmmm, hmmmmmmmming. These are actually the opening notes to Beethoven's fifth symphony without the first note. Think about it.

When the meerkats are pups, the researchers handle them a lot, and as soon as they can eat solid food, they feed them hard-boiled eggs, because they like them, and offer water from bottles with sippy tubes. Because of this training, they can now weigh them three times a day. Habituating is not the same as taming. The animals only tolerate humans to get the egg and the water.

When most of them had emerged, our researcher got out a scale and a plastic box, scooped a little sand into the box, recalibrated the scale, and pulled out a water bottle and a small plastic box of crumbled hard-boiled egg. Then she called "yum-yum, yum-yum" in a cute little voice, as if she were tempting a toddler to eat. She offered them water or egg, and one by one got them into the tray and weighed them. Then she wrote the weight in a battered book using a pencil on a string. It looked odd, with all the electronic equipment otherwise being used;

yet somewhat comforting to know that scientists are still using the methods of the earliest observers.

If the meerkats wouldn't get on the scale and she could not reach them, she sometimes picked them up by the base of the tail and placed them in the box. Those who wanted more treats, and tried to get into the box with one already being weighed, were gently pushed aside with the back of her other hand. There was no grabbing: that would have ruined all the habituation work. Besides, they bite, and their claws are sharp.

Eventually, the group started foraging and roaming around. At some point, they all put their tails in the air and took off running. We got a call on the radio that another group was headed for this one. The Whiskers group took off in that direction and began war dancing, which is a hop into the air while running. Away they went, and we followed. They arrived at the burrow where the other meerkats had been, and ran around, marking everything. Meerkats have really stinky anal glands that do the trick. They also urinate and poop near the burrow openings, and our leader took samples in little plastic bags. These

Meerkats huddled against the cold (courtesy Ellen Westbrook).

Meerkats are coaxed to the scales and weighed twice a day (courtesy Ellen Westbrook).

would later be frozen and sent to Cambridge in England, where they would be analyzed by some poor graduate student, no doubt.

When the meerkats are running, they run in bursts, stop, and become vigilant. That is, they stand tippy-toe on their hind legs, using their tails as support, and look for predators. Then they run some more. Some "guard" by climbing a bush or tree or fence or even a sitting human, and stand up and look around. Among other things, they are looking for predatory birds so high in the air that my puny eyes could only sometimes find a speck.

While we walked around watching them forage, one caught a lizard and had to fight to keep it. If there are pups in the group, they wander around foraging, but also making a high-pitched feeding call. Sometimes an adult will give a pup something they've caught. The pups tend to play and tussle a lot. We asked about the size of prey meerkats could take down and were told someone had seen them mob and kill a rabbit. They surrounded it, got hold of it, and tore it apart.

Meerkats scramble up anything to look for danger. This is called guarding behavior.

After a couple of hours, we went back to the farmhouse and then shuttled back to our place to eat lunch. While there, I washed out some clothes and hung them on the line on the porch. At least the porch protected the laundry from the larger wildlife. The researchers have had eland strolling through their clotheslines and walking off with underwear hooked on their horns.

At 3:00 p.m., we met outside (too cold in the main house) and learned to use GPS devices. We also learned about poisonous snakes and scorpions. The younger half of our team of six had the GPS down in no time. I was pushing buttons and wishing I had my brother's techno-wizard brain for a minute so that I could figure it out. However, when we handed off the gadgets to each other to follow what we'd put into them, the one I programmed worked, and the one I had been given didn't work because the kid screwed up. Ha! Old lady revenge!

We were free 'til dinner and had no idea how lucky we were. The researchers were easing us into this. In our *rondavels* was a backpack containing a clipboard, first-aid kit (those pesky snakes), pen, pencil, eraser, and a big fat field guide. I looked at the manual and started to realize how complicated this was. Oh no, could I do this? Did I want to do this? I was a 67-year-old lady far from home. I began to wonder why I had thought this was a good idea.

We went to the farmhouse for dinner with all the students and scientists. A tour of the place revealed room after room of computer equipment and dusty backpacks and electronic equipment, all that scientific junk you find in a field research site. They had a fire going in their little stove in the corner of the living room (lounge) and a makeshift table-and-bench arrangement stuffed into the middle. We all crowded in and feasted on salad and game pie. The latter was made of large chunks of eland meat and an occasional hunk of orange winter squash covered by a three-inch biscuity crust—yum, yum. Dessert, or pudding, was a very moist cake sort of thing with a lot of brown sugar in it.

I sat next to a married couple doing research on babblers, which are pretty little white birds with black tails and wingtips. The man was very persistent with questions, and I was feeling tired, stressed, and, well, cranky, and I believe I said something a bit rude. He was going on about science and discoveries, all very romantic stuff that sounded like something Mr. Rogers might tell the kids. Then he said that all the animals out there in the Kalahari understood each other's languages, their calls. I said, "Why would you think they didn't?" Then we discussed how some science is just proving things. Uh-oh, I hoped I wasn't getting sick. When I don't feel well, I tend to think everyone I come into contact with is an IDIOT and say the wrong things.

We saw lots of animals on the drive over, and on the way back, Melissa held a spotlight out the window, and we saw more, including blue wildebeests under a tree, bush hare—and spring hare, which were really odd. They jump like a wallaby and have long bushy tails like a fox, but they are rabbits. Once home, I braved a shower in the frigid bath block, as I had sand coming out of my ears and off my eyebrows.

We were warned that the pipes might freeze, so we filled our electric kettles before going to bed. As Ellen had no clock, and I feared I wouldn't hear the one I had brought, she took mine. Each morning, she came to my hut and knocked at just before six, when the sky was still paved with starlight.

The next morning, it was below freezing again, and I woke with a sore throat and a throbbing headache. I took acetaminophen. I thought it might be a sinus problem due to the dry air and dust. Hoped it wasn't a cold. The grouchy old lady still stared back from the mirror.

That morning, I was with a different researcher and group of volunteers, and we went to a different meerkat mob, which needed to be found with VHF. While the researcher was weighing them, several lined up along her leg and thigh, stood up, and leaned back against her to stay warm. I wished I could do the same. When they took off, they decided to cross a road, and we got to climb our first fences. The first was two meters high. Up and over the top we went in our winter duds, boots, and backpack. Not hard except for the wire on our hands, which is why we were told to bring work gloves. Later, the meerkats decided to come back, and we needed to go over fences again. They scooted right through at the bottom, of course.

We saw drongos, small black birds that follow meerkats and try to steal their food. These birds perch on grasses and bushes near the foraging meerkats. When a meerkat seems to have found something delicious, the drongo flutters in and hovers about 18 inches above the meerkat, ready to snatch the find. They came within touching distance of us and are beautiful. Of course, the meerkats aren't above attacking a drongo.

Back to the house for lunch, one egg over easy with toast and jam, a banana and tea. I washed some more clothes by hand and hung them out, heeding the sign on the front door saying to keep it closed so that the ground squirrels didn't come inside.

That afternoon, we learned to do foraging focals—one of the research methods I read about in the handbook that made me doubt my abilities. A focal consists of two people with stopwatches and one with a clipboard and tally sheet. After the meerkats have been weighed and 50 percent of them have begun foraging, the two people find the meerkat they are to follow. The meerkats are marked with black hair dye. The researcher uses a long, flat artist's paintbrush and quietly follows the animals, then reaches down and daubs a little dye on marks that are fading. The meerkats don't like it and evade them.

Finding the meerkats in the morning with technology (courtesy Ellen West-brook).

Ellen held the clipboard, and I watched the meerkat. When we spotted the one we needed and it began foraging, we both started our stopwatches. While hers would continue to run for 15 minutes, I started and stopped mine every time the meerkat started and stopped foraging. We soon found out we didn't really know what foraging was. They started digging, and sand flew through their back legs, but then they quit in a matter of seconds. Was that a dig or not? Oh, and did I mention that we were supposed to write down what they got and what size it was? Yes, lizards (easy), scorpions (easy), spiders, grubs, ants, and beetles (not so easy). And most of them are eaten while the meerkat has his head down the hole.

We thought we were failing miserably at focals. Our researcher *du jour* was of no help, as he had never done them. He was busy walking around with a hand-held electronic data-collecting thingy and punching buttons. Hmmm, hmmm, hmmmmmm. He was easy on the eyes, and when he crouched to weigh the animals, we could see that he was

134

wearing black underwear. The young single women—who had worked with him out here in the middle of nowhere for a year—must have noticed him in spades if the grouchy old lady did.

When the meerkats headed for the burrows for the evening, we all followed. They were weighed— while we all got colder and colder. Finally, the meerkats went down the burrow and off to bed for the night, because they were cold, too. We headed back to the ranch and supper, which was some kind of mince (hamburger) cooked up with tasty sauce and homemade buns. Melissa said they were like fry bread, only they were puffy and light and bready, and we sliced them and made sloppy joes. Then we hung around and talked with our two guests from the researchers' house.

Because four people got shocked while they were showering the night before, I decided to just wash up in the sink and go to bed. I was still not feeling well and was taking pills. I put on all my usual bedclothes and got into bed with my hot water bottle. Blessings on the head of the person who put the hot water bottles in the *rondavels*.

The next morning, Ellen knocked on the door, and I dreaded getting up. Although I had kept the heater on day and night—even when it warmed up during the day—it was still freezing in the *rondavel* when I arose. Still, I couldn't tell if I was sick or allergic. My nose was running and raw; my attitude was awful. I was convinced that everyone was dumber than a box of rocks and that I had made a big mistake coming here. I counted the days until I could go home. I thought about begging off and staying in bed, but that would have been so boring, and practically as cold as everything else. The previous night, the water lines in some of the *rondavels* had frozen. I said the prayer of the intrepid, "Oh, well."

The next morning, I was in a group that went back to the meerkats we saw to bed the night before. We all stood outside the burrows— freezing. My nose was dripping like a faucet; my pockets were stuffed with soaking tissues and toilet paper. The meerkats finally emerged and stood looking at us while we hummed a little here and there. Slowly, they began to wander around. One came over, looked up at me, and then parked himself on my boot, which must have been a little warmer than the sand. Then he decided to play with my shoelaces. Hmm, I touched my shoelaces. Some of the meerkats have TB. Alternative: "Oh, well."

The dominant male in this group of meerkats was named Finn McCool, and he was vicious. Finn wanted the water but hated the bottle and attacked it with claws and teeth. Once the meerkats were weighed, they took off, and we followed—over fences and into a goat and sheep yard filled with pellets, commonly known as goat shit. Then across another fence, then another. Ellen and I were doing foraging focals with the stopwatches and the clipboard, and my nose was dripping. When we finished, and were just standing around and following meerkats, I held my wet tissues off my fingers like flags to dry them so I could use them again.

When we got back for lunch, I took an antihistamine, acetaminophen, and a throat lozenge and hoped for the best. Then we sat outside and learned about the birds we would be looking for in the field. In the afternoon, the weather warmed up and was pleasant. Then we went out and practiced what we had learned about the birds, which was not nearly as tiring as the foraging focal business—many fences to climb.

As the meerkats were gathering at their burrow for the night,

Weigh-in, loving that water (courtesy Ellen Westbrook).

a lone female came down the road and warily watched them. It was sunset, and we were pulling on our jackets. Instead of heading down the burrow holes, however, the meerkats piled together in a shivering mass, trying to stay warm—but they were still keeping an eye on the intruder. Then, one after another, they headed down to their beds. When the last one went down, the intruder stealthily headed for one of the other openings and went down, too. She was an evicted female. She might be let back in if she was lucky. The dominant female in each group evicts females who get pregnant. The stress to these cooperative animals of being on their own usually causes them to abort. The females try to come back, or sometimes they hook up with a roving male and form a new colony.

The shower was still shocking people, so I declined again. The youngest two of us, just graduated high school, thought it some kind of sport and were having a jolly good time at it. I still couldn't seem to get warm. The witch in the mirror was beginning to look like she might have an escape plan.

Finally, the next morning, I was feeling a bit better and finding out how sick I must have been by comparison. I felt like I had come out of a cloudbank. My nose didn't run anymore, and those people weren't the idiots they were until yesterday. I had really been out of it. Now I was beginning to just look around with wonder. Sure, it was still cold in the morning and at night, but this was the Kalahari. Sometimes when we were in a place away from roads and buildings—and that was often—you could look all around and see nothing but land and sky. It was like being at sea without the water.

One morning, on GPS duty, I really needed to go to the bathroom. Finally, I said I was going to the ladies' room and pointed uphill towards a tree, which I thought was remote enough for privacy. I got up there, dug a hole in the sand, pulled down my layers of pants, and squatted. Just then, a flock of babblers, birds I hadn't yet seen, came flying into the low-branched tree just over my head. I could have reached up and touched one. They are very pretty, but I wondered if they were attracted by what I was contributing to the desert floor.

I got my pants up and was kicking sand like my cat does when I saw the meerkats and the humans headed my way. That was close. As for the babblers, I found out later they had been habituated to come to someone in a squatting position so they could be weighed and given treats for cooperating.

After a while, when we were almost finished for the morning, I decided to rest by sitting on the ground with my legs straight out in front of me, my pack still on my back. I took some pictures, then felt and heard claws scrabbling up my backpack. I was going to be used as a guard station, except whoever it was couldn't get enough purchase to climb me and fell off.

Back for lunch. People were working on the electrical problem so we wouldn't get shocked when we took showers and washed the dishes. Hard to do dishes when you're afraid of the water.

In the afternoon, the three youngest of the group were taken to a group of meerkats in the ostrich field, so named because a male ostrich guards it and likes to attack people. Well, the ostrich spotted them and headed their way. Their researcher told them to run for the fence. They had to sprint about 150 meters to the fence through sand. They clambered over and escaped with the ostrich about ten feet behind them.

At dinner, Melissa said the ostrich treed one of the researchers once, and she had to go in with a vehicle and get between the ostrich and the tree the researcher had climbed. After getting the researcher inside, she said, the ostrich stood in front of the vehicle, and she drove slowly forward and pushed it. He acted as if he were ready to take on the truck.

I was not going to that field.

Finally, a day off. I didn't get up until the sun was well-risen and then took my time having breakfast. I washed my jeans from last week and my goin' home pants and hung them out. Then, around 2:00 p.m., it was time to go on a game ride. We all piled into a truck. We had been told to bring binoculars and cameras, but I forgot my camera. The truck had roll bars (my hand barely made it around), which we held onto as we stood in the back. Off we went, heaving and dipping like we were on a boat in heavy seas. When game was spotted, I would hit the roof of the cab with my hand, and Melissa would stop. We would count the animals and record them: many springbok, a few great hulking blue wildebeests, elegant red hartebeests, eland, and bat-eared foxes. The most beautiful animal for me was the gemsbok, or oryx gazelle, a large brown animal with black-and-white markings on its face and legs, with long, slightly curving horns, and with a black tail like a horse's. To see these animals standing and running through the grass is so unlike seeing them in zoos. They are so much more beautiful in their environment in the clear air under an African sun.

An interesting part of this adventure was the speed of the learning. We were instructed for what seemed like too brief a time on a research method that seemed quite complicated. Then we were taken out, and we did it. We began the next day late, at 8:00 a.m., by learning about biodiversity surveys. Then we saddled up and headed out. We worked in pairs, and as soon as Melissa felt we were all competent, she drove away and left us to make our way through the desert in different directions. I worked the GPS, kept us on the route, and took location sightings as we found the plants and animals we sought. Ellen recorded more data on paper forms, and together we looked for details, such as how many white-browed sparrow nests are in a tree and how many of them are for sleeping (two holes) and mating (one hole) and the like.

It was just lovely being out there, just the two of us figuring it out. Was it a camelthorn tree or a grey camelthorn tree?—a burrow or just a hole in the ground?—a rat's nest or just a bunch of sticks? The easiest ones were the invasive mesquite and Mexican poppy, the latter all in seedpods and very striking. Occasionally, we found a thornless shrub—that's the raisin bush. Eventually, we got to the end of our search, which was also a fence line, and wondered which way to go to meet the others. Finally, we called Melissa on the radio, and she came and picked us up. We were the last two of the six to finish, but we also tracked closest to the prescribed route. Besides, it was just too pretty out there to rush.

Back at the ranch, Ellen and I entered our data into the computer and then ate lunch. I made myself a nice scrambled egg sandwich with Wellington's Sweet Chili Sauce—I did like that stuff. We had the afternoon off—I loved the laziness. Then we went out to the dunes for sundowners—which consisted of a cup of South African creamy liqueur, Doritos and peanuts. We sat and chatted and took pictures and had a lovely time, then headed back for a dinner of fajitas, of all things.

Back on our early schedule the next day, we were in the truck by seven and headed for our groups. The light was like clear water. The sun was blazing as if there were little atmosphere to filter it. And of course, the sun shone every day. It wasn't going to rain, that's for sure. The temperature rose dramatically, and I ended up removing both jackets and my sweater as well as my rain pants and thought eagerly of taking off my extra heavy socks and undershirt when I got back. When the sun began to set, however, I dug into my pack and found my sweater and fleece jacket again.

Dinner was *boerewors, pap, sous* and gem squash, Afrikaans dishes. The *boerewors* turned out to be sausages. The *pap* is cornmeal-like stuff that is white and not like corn, good but hard to explain—maybe a heavy version of grits. The *sous* is a sauce that is tomato-based and quite good. The squash is like tiny acorn squashes, cut in half to form little cups that were roasted in the oven and had some kind of seasoning in them. There was a black woman who came and cooked sometimes, and that day she seemed to be cleaning the kitchen and dining area quite thoroughly. I believe she preferred Afrikaans to English. She had quite a good glare, a natural African power *pani*.

We got to sleep a little later the next morning, as we went out at eight o'clock instead of seven to do a vegetation survey. At least it was daylight when I headed for the house. As usual, I went into the kitchen, thinking, "What shall I have? Something different." I ended up with that damned muesli with some spoonfuls of yogurt. The yogurt was good, but the muesli was dry and uninteresting, so I scraped it into the bucket that went to the chickens and made myself peanut butter toast.

Somewhere, we pulled off the road, and Melissa grabbed a coil of string and a bunch of what looked like meter-long pieces of rebar. She set one of the rods into the ground, quite easy in this sand, and then attached a string to it and started backing up. In the end, she had marked off a quadrant containing four plots, measuring 10 meters by 20 meters. We paired up and recorded 200 points within these areas, noting plant species and growth form. I walked around with the stick calling things out, and Ellen wrote it down. Thank goodness there was little variety, or we would have been up the creek. Mainly, there was sour grass, a small shrub known as three thorn, and some larger shrub that we found difficult to name, even after searching for it in the book. Our work didn't take long, and the weather was pleasant.

We had a little talk from one of the researchers and learned more about the meerkats. They are officially *Suricata suricatta*. Their cooperative behavior helps the group to become larger, which makes them stronger and better able to fight off predators, yields greater pup size (more feeders), and enables them to win more inter-group interactions. The cooperative behavior includes babysitting, when the pups are still in the burrow, and also pup feeding and guarding. As I often saw cows babysitting back home, I asked about the difference and learned that cows are social animals, which are different from cooperative animals. The latter put their lives at risk to help the group. Helpers sacrifice weight, for instance, because they can't be out foraging solely for themselves.

The next day we visited a school in a town called Vanzylsrus. The town is tiny, and the school contains grades one through eight. There was a large poster in the lobby explaining what abuse is—from bullies, parents, strangers, and police—and what one should do about it. It also explained rights. There was lots of artwork, and there were curtains, made not of lace as in Eastern European schools, but of bright, cheerful cotton.

We were greeted by a teacher who took us to her class of third-graders, about 30 of them in blue-and-grey uniforms. We introduced ourselves and pointed on the world map to show them where we lived and told them what it is like there and what we did.

From there, we went to the main office and sat at a table. We had a delicious tea made from the rooibos bush, one I needed to get to take home. Then we went to another building, which contained the art classroom. I walked around and looked at the supplies. They had some enamel house paint, large jars of tempera powder, and a box of small watercolor tins licked nearly clean of paint. Then we went to one of the temporary buildings, where an older class sang a couple of those African-style songs (like the ones you hear on Paul Simon albums) and the national anthem. Finally, we were taken back to the entrance and thanked profusely for our gifts. I had brought a backpack filled with construction and drawing paper, pencils, crayons, paint boxes, etc.

Then we went a block or two to the only hotel in town, where we had lunch. The restaurant was outlandishly decorated with chartreuse dining room walls and bright red curtains. The bathroom was worth the trip—hot pink walls, fancy doodads everywhere, and butterflies in the clear plastic toilet seat. We were greeted by a pudgy Dachshund named Fudge. After we ate, we browsed the gift shop. I bought two bundles of 16-inch-long porcupine quills and some cards with meerkats on them. Ellen and I also went down the street to the store, a place to buy anything and everything. I ended up with the last dusty box of rooibos tea. The liquor store was the last stop. I decided I would break my dry spell and went in. Everything was in a caged area behind the counter. There didn't seem to be any wine, and I didn't want liquor, so I bought the creamy South African liqueur. Along the way back to our base, I spotted huge birds, somewhere between the size of an ostrich and a crane. They were brown and had crowns on their heads. Melissa said they are called bustards.

That afternoon, Ellen and I were with the meerkat group called the Aztecs. Our researcher drove us out to where she thought the meerkats might be. Once we got there, we hunted and hunted for a signal from the dominant female's radio collar, hiking up and down dunes through scrub until we finally found the mob and set to work. Ellen and I were researching the birds, which was easy as there weren't many of them. When the sun began to set, the meerkats took off and ended up at a burrow they seemed to like. Weighing began. The day was winding down. Then three or four of them wandered off and became vigilant; then, a few more joined them.

The next thing we knew, they were all off and running through the grass. We grabbed the equipment and hustled after them, and finally, they came upon another burrow. The weighing began again—but wait a minute. This wasn't the burrow they wanted, either, so back they ran in the opposite direction. The meerkats dashed back and forth, here and there, and finally settled on a burrow and went down for the night, lickety-split.

Then we had to get back to the truck. We had a GPS setting for it, so that wasn't a problem, but the sun had set, and it was getting dark quickly. We set off at a rapid pace and got there while we could still somewhat see where we were going. The moon was bright, but the holes were deep. I rode in the back of the truck and collected my Kalahari soul souvenir, rocking down a sand road in the moonlight, the desert stretching out forever. I was astonished at how fortunate I was to be at that spot on the planet.

Another early morning, we were ready to roll by seven o'clock and headed out, only to find that we needed to wait forever for the meerkats to get up. I had all my warm clothing on, but by noon, I had shed as much as I could. It was actually hot. All was going incredibly boringly. Then, while doing the lunchtime weighing of the meerkats, Finn McCool bit the researcher's thumb. We rummaged through all our first-aid kits, and she bandaged herself up. Then we slogged back to the truck, which must have been a mile away. We finally got back for lunch. While helping Ellen do dishes, she mentioned that she ate half the leftover dessert and that I should grab the other half. It was one of those puddings that is actually a very moist cake. I poured custard over it and scarfed it down. Yum-yum. That night before dinner, I sipped my liqueur while writing up what had happened during the day. Before I knew it, I had a buzz. Not what I wanted to happen. I took the bottle to the kitchen and left it for others.

I finally turned off the heater the next morning, and after lunch, I found that the room was warm. In fact, the walls were warm to the touch. We had clouds for the first time, and the sky so vast it looked as if there were enough clouds to blanket the entire state of Texas.

Our last time with the meerkats, I was with the Aztec group, and the meerkats were frisky and cute while they were being weighed. Since it was Sunday, we had the afternoon off and prepared for our departure the next morning. The day was spent packing, reading, knitting and watching birds with Ellen on the front porch. There was a faucet in the yard with a constant drip, and the birds came to drink from it. There were flocks of white eyebrow sociable weavers and babblers, as well as canaries and some birds we had never seen before, including one with a beautiful lavender head and red beak. While we watched, two ground squirrels ran about across the road, and a badger and mongoose came and went. Early to bed since wake-up was 5:15 a.m.

We rose in the dark, had a hasty breakfast, loaded our bags into the trailer behind the Land Rover, and piled in. I got the front seat again and got to see the animals crossing the road in the dark—and then the roadkill—as the sky lightened on the drive to Upington. At one point, I saw two animals cross the road and wondered what they were. If anyone would know, it would be our driver, Melissa, who said, "What the hell is that?" as she braked and pulled over. She jumped out and dove into the brush to figure out what they were. We all piled out to stretch our legs and admire her bravery—there were snakes in there. What she thought might have been cheetah cubs turned out to be jackals. We loaded up and got going again.

In Upington, we waited at the small airport and then finally boarded the first leg home. On the tarmac, we were each given a fortune-cookie-sized slip of paper. Unfolded, I found this joke, "My wife has a slight impediment in her speech. Every now and then she stops to breathe. – Jimmy Durante." No one was laughing. In a couple of hours, we landed in Johannesburg, where we had an eight-hour layover. Fortunately, the airport is large and has interesting shops and restaurants. We hung out, sauntered around, and eventually got to our gate, where we hung out and sauntered some more. Finally, we boarded the plane for our 18-hour flight.

In Atlanta, I collected my bags, hugged Ellen good-bye, went through customs, and rechecked my bag. Then I headed for the next gate, where I called Wally. It was the first time I'd talked with him since I had left 20 days before. It was heaven to hear his voice. He was heading for the local airport to pick me up, and I was headed for the plane to get there.

Always wonderful to get back home—but so hot in July.

11

Easter Island, Examining Stone Heads— Age 68 (2011)

Another year older and time to hit the road again. Ellen thought Easter Island needed our attention. While flying more than 2,300 miles west over the Pacific from Santiago, Chile, to meet her there, I watched a documentary on the plane. A native of the island laughed when he explained that they were survivors—after all, they knew how to eat people to stay alive. I hadn't found that expressed in the books and scientific papers recommended by Earthwatch to prepare for this trip. I had read about cannibalism in the island's past but had never thought of it as a survival skill. But of course, it is.

After almost six hours of flying, people began to gape out the port-side windows, and I was able to glimpse a bit of land. The plane seemed to take forever to line up with the runway. I mean, it is the only thing out there. What was the pilot waiting for? I began to wonder if we were soon going to scoop fishes when we finally landed. There was plenty of runway, as the United States had expanded it in the 1980s so the Space Shuttle could land there if necessary. Soon, Ellen was calling my name. She had arrived the day before. Then one of our leaders was putting a lei around my neck, as I was welcomed to Rapa Nui, the real name of the island that is one of the most remote inhabited places on earth. It's true that Bhutan, where I went on a tour, is remote, situated in the Himalayas, and the isolation we had in the Kalahari made it seem remote. But in both cases, a person could actually drive or even walk away to another place from there. Not so from here.

The first clue that I was going somewhere vastly different from other places I had visited was on the luggage carrousel. The plane, because of the distance, was large, but unlike the usual boring rounds of luggage and sporting equipment at the carousel, it was more like bus cargo. Because it is the only way people of Rapa Nui get back and forth to the mainland, the plane carries the kinds of things you would normally stuff into your car to go to Grandma's house. There were cardboard boxes strapped with rope, Styrofoam coolers slathered with duct tape, all stuffed with goodies hard to get on the island—like apples, shoes, and car parts. Going in the other direction, from the island, were homegrown avocados, papaya, bananas, and guava, and maybe some purple sweet potatoes and carrots the size of eggplants.

The island is a mere 66 square miles and is guarded by its reef-less coast. It is true that cruise ships now visit, but there is no port for large vessels. Only if the ocean is cooperative may passengers go by tender to the island. Only then can they enjoy the sights for which the island is famous: the *moai*, the great stone heads that stare across the landscape, their backs turned to the pounding Pacific.

Easter Island, named for the day it was "discovered" by Dutch Commander Jacob Roggeveen, on April 5, 1722, is also known as Isla de Pascua in Spanish. The island is a special territory of Chile. But the people who somehow came to find this island in the vast Pacific Ocean, and made it their home, call it Rapa Nui. They discovered it more than 700 years before Commander Roggeveen arrived with his three ships.

As a member of a seven-person team (five American women, one Australian man, and one British woman), I worked with archeologists for two weeks and learned far more than I dreamed possible. I found out that when the first plane landed on the island, people thought it was a big bird that was going to eat them. Before that plane, the island was served by one supply ship a year. And until the 1960s, the surviving Rapa Nui people were confined to the settlement of Hanga Roa, and the rest of the island was rented to the Williamson-Balfour Company as a sheep farm until 1953. After that, the island was managed by the Chilean Navy until 1966, and at that point, the rest of the island was reopened.

As it turned out, our team leaders, both of Rapa Nui descent, told us of the days before electricity. One told us how her parents took her to tour that once-a-year ship. She was excited and was soon running around the decks alone. When she began to search for her parents, she discovered not only were they not on board, but also that her island home was getting smaller and smaller as she sailed for Valparaiso. They had tricked her into leaving home for her education. She was 12 years old and doesn't remember what happened that first year, except that approaching the coastline of Chile at night, she thought the stars had fallen close to the water. It was her first view of a city lighted by electricity. Her father came at the end of that first year to find out how she was doing. He decided she was depending too much on the Rapa Nui community in Valparaiso, so he put her in a school in southern Chile. Isolated, she gained her education. Now grown up, Sonoa Haoa Cardinali is in charge of the island's national monuments. When we were there, she was surveying the island's archeological sites. She was our boss.

Today, the sheep and the fences are gone, and polite dogs and horses amble, at their leisure, through the streets, yards, and fields of the island. The dogs know everyone on the island and easily spot tourists. They saunter across the street and park themselves near newcomers, waiting to find out if a dog lover might have a tasty tidbit or an ear scratch. The only time they seem rambunctious is when they are playing with each other and competing to raise a leg and mark the door to the Internet café. The Rapa Nui people ignore their antics, which must account for their polite behavior. They all appear to be well-fed and healthy, and during afternoon siesta, when many shops close, they can be seen stretched out snoozing in the sun. The horses have the same run of the place, and people erect fences to keep them out of their gardens. The horses, like the dogs, have owners.

Chickens run around as well, scratching the earth for grubs. A couple of roosters served as our alarm clocks when we stayed at a sort of hotel that was built for some German archeologists to use when they are on the island to work. One hen appeared every few days with her chicks to search the flower beds for food, and a family of feral cats peeked into the kitchen when they could and occasionally looked longingly through the dining room door while we feasted on fresh—well, fresh everything. Our cook was a young woman whose children sometimes ran around the place as carefree and mom-dependent as the chicks. We had fresh avocado at every meal and plenty of papayas. We stuffed ourselves but didn't gain weight. I think it was the lack of frying and the general absence of fatty foods—plus our work every day.

To introduce us to the island, we were taken on a walking tour of Hanga Roa. The tiny waterfront sported a saint's shrine and colorful boats in water so clear, but for the sunlight reflecting off the surface, it was transparent. The adjoining park contains fine examples of *moai* on their platforms, known as *ahu*, as well as house ruins, a cave, and the ever-present and the not-to-be-ignored Pacific Ocean. The park has stone walls at one end and a heavy metal pipe turnstile, not to control crowds or collect tickets, but rather, to keep out the horses. Inside the enclosure, we found a large pig securely tied to a tree with a rope. This was our first glimpse of those famous statues rising into the sky, their backs to the crashing waves. They stare a little skyward, still, but for the small birds landing on their faces to make flickering eyelashes for them with their feathers.

All too soon, the touring was over, and we were put to work, part

Our hotel courtyard where the chickens and their chicks hung out (courtesy Louise Jones-Takata).

of which was being useful at the national nursery where research is going on in reforestation. We weeded pots of small trees, filled bags with potting soil, and transplanted tree seedlings. Ellen and I transplanted more than 1,500 of those one-inch plants the first day on the job. It helps to be a bit compulsive. There is evidence that the island

Rapa Nui beach (courtesy Louise Jones-Takata).

once was forested with a hardy palm that has disappeared. How and why that happened is one of the many mysteries of Rapa Nui.

A great deal of literature about the island and its people contains the word *mystery* in the title. Where did the people come from? Why did they build the *moai*? How did they transport them from the quarry where they were made to the seaside? Why did they later knock them

The author weeding at the forestry department (courtesy Louise Jones-Takata).

down? Researchers theorize and experiment, run tests, and write papers.

What I can tell you is that there are far more *moai* on the island than those seen on postcards. One conservative estimate has it between 800 and a thousand of the giant statues, and no two appear to be exactly alike. As for why the Rapa Nui people carved them—this is not an answer I was burning to know. I appreciate them and don't need to know the "why." I've always thought that people who lived before the development of a lot of handy technology were not stupid for not having it—and casting about for their methods as though they were handicapped by their time period has always seemed condescending to me.

Our archeological work in the field consisted of two tasks, for which we were split into teams. After a drive out into the rolling hills and bumping down a rough road, we would head out on foot to work with four young researchers. Four of our group went to a pile of rocks that turned out to be a site where *moai* once stood. At first, it all looked like rubble, and then, with experience, sure enough, we could see one of the huge statues face down in the dirt. Someone needed to get down there and measure his nose. I was in a team of three that struck out cross country and found sites of ancient houses, rock gardens, and what are called chicken houses. These are windowless rock structures that are said once to have housed chickens. The theory was that at night, one removed a strategic rock and stuffed the chickens inside, then recapped it to keep them safe. There was no mortar, so air was not a problem. Perhaps they were chicken houses; perhaps they had another use. The jury is still out on that one.

It was winter, and the grasses were dry and golden. It seemed as though the entire area was covered with loose, black volcanic rock hidden in all that grass—real ankle busters. I was very glad I had brought my collapsible hiking stick. And always, just over a hill or around a turn, there was that magnificent ocean flaunting its blueness at the sky. The sites we would come upon looked to me like any old heap of rocks. Sonia was the person who saw what all the other archeologists who came to the island missed. These rocks were not a natural and random dispersion. They had been placed there by people working the land. She or her young helpers would walk about and plant little flags on sticks where they discovered significant pieces among this rubble. Then we would be told what these things were: earth ovens, house ruins, *buros* (rocks tumbled by the ocean), or rock gardens. Because there is and was very little water on the island, ancient people placed rocks to conserve any moisture that came along as the rocks kept moisture from quickly evaporating from the soil. Whereas we would consider a rock garden as mainly composed of plants with rocks for accent, these rock gardens are the opposite. Many had ferns growing in them, and some had long vines of some kind of squash, "like little pumpkins," our researcher explained. We were told that tests revealed this method of growing was efficient. Although fewer plants were grown because of the space taken by the rocks, the plants were higher in nutrients than those grown without the rocks.

Once we arrived at a flag, our leader would take a GPS siting and then commence entering the answers to nearly 20 questions about the site into the same hand-held device. Ellen placed a wooden arrow-shaped marker onto the site, oriented north, and took pictures of it. I drew the site, and also marked north on my drawing. The third volunteer measured the site and called out the numbers to our leader. Then we would scramble off to the next place.

At noon, we would settle down for the lunch each of us had packed after breakfast and chat with our young hosts or learn from our leader. The young women working with her brought plastic boxes of cold spaghetti, onto which they would pour a freshly opened can of mussels or fish as a sauce. After our work was finished around four in the afternoon, we would hike back to the trucks, meet up with the other group, and head back to town. One day, we got stuck in a rainstorm at least a mile out from the trucks. The young women who led us offered to get the truck and bring it closer to us, but we said not to bother: we were already soaked. We all took off through the wet, hip-high weeds. My rain jacket kept me fairly dry, but my heavy work pants were soaked, and my hiking boots were sloshing. I had lent my rain pants to one of the girls to cover her shoulders. Since things dried slowly in our rooms, I had a dip in morale that night as I lay in bed and thought about going back out with damp pants and wet boots the next day.

Happily, it didn't rain the following day, and I was able to layer some comfortable, lightweight-but-dry pants under the returned rain gear. Ellen, ever resourceful, had brought a plastic laundry bag, and we cut it into four equal sheets and wrapped our socked feet with it before putting on our wet boots. My feet were warmer and drier than they had been since I got there. This traveler will be packing a plastic garbage bag for her next trip. The other team told us they had made a dash for the trucks when it started to rain (they were closer) only to find them locked. Their leaders led them to a cave with an opening slightly larger than a pair of middle-aged hips and urged them to go down. One person, afraid of enclosed spaces, stayed out. One who went in later described the experience as part *Alice in Wonderland* and part hell, with an emphasis on the latter. Yet, Rapa Nui people had lived in caves. With little wood with which to build, it was a natural alternative.

We were just part of a long line of investigators on Rapa Nui. The island has been under scrutiny since that Dutch sailing party went ashore and wrote about their observations. They could not figure out how the natives could have erected those huge figures with their big, staring eyes and red hats. Weighing between 14 and 30 tons and standing 14 to 30 feet tall, how had they carved them without metal tools—and moved with without wheels or beasts of burden? The Europeans, having all these things, were baffled.

Come to find out, they did the carving using tools made of basalt, which is solidified lava that is harder than the volcanic tuff from which the statues are carved. We found one of these tools in the field one day. I thought we would take it back to the office, but no, our researcher merely tucked it into a pile of stones in the grass and left it there. It seemed a respectful act. As I did more archaeological work, I would learn that this was standard practice, but it hadn't always been.

The scientific study of Easter Island began with Captain James Cook's visit in 1774. Cook was not looking for this island. According to John Flenley and Paul Bahn's book, *The Enigmas of Easter Island*, Cook and his crew were ill from the rigors of sailing beyond the Antarctic Circle—upon the first ship to go there. They came upon Easter Island and received food from the natives and also traded with them. Early archeological work was conducted by Germans in 1882 and then by an American team in 1886. Unlike previous visitors, who spent mere days on the island, a lone Englishwoman, Mrs. Katherine Routledge, lived there for 17 months in the early 1900s.

Work continued through the decades. However, it took Thor Heyerdahl and his raft, Kon Tiki, to bring the area to broad public attention. A Norwegian scientist, Thor Heyerdahl, theorized Peruvian natives had populated the Pacific islands. To test his theory, Heyerdahl and five of his friends traveled to Peru in 1947. There they replicated a balsa wood raft that they thought was like the early versions used by Indians. They were 101 days at sea before arriving at Raroia in French Polynesia. The men recorded their journey with a movie camera and later produced the film, *Kon Tiki*. After its release in 1950, it won an Academy Award for documentary film. The win put the theory and the adventure squarely in the public's mind.

Since then, Heyerdahl's premise, that the island was settled by Native Americans from the coast of South America, has been disproved by DNA testing of ancient remains. The island was settled by Polynesians. However, its remoteness offers a laboratory of sorts for researchers in a variety of areas. Carbon dating has revealed that the island has been occupied since 380 CE. There is the question as to why the vast forests that existed in the past disappeared. Long-gone plant life can be identified from pollen samples deep in the mud of the crater lakes. The island once was a haven for seabirds, but we saw only two bird species, sparrow and hawk. Some theorize the birds were all eaten. There are no native land vertebrates. Rabbits were introduced in 1866, but the people ate them all by 1911. The population was once about 15,000, a number far too large for the island to sustain. Eventually, the population dropped to a mere 111 people, thanks to the crews of Western ships, who kidnapped inhabitants and returned people infected with smallpox. Old sculptures depict skeletal humans. And, when food is too scarce, survival can include cannibalism, an acknowledged part of Rapa Nui history—and the explanation for the comment on that documentary I watched on the plane. One of the easily found tourist sites is Ana Kai Tangata, a seaside cavern with impressive rock art on its ceiling. The ambiguous name of the cave could mean "cave where men eat," "cave where men are eaten," or "cave that eats men."

Speaking of eating, one day, heading out to the field, we rode with a man we hadn't met before. On the way, we stopped at his house and picked up a supply of lemons. Then we stopped along the way near a stand of Eucalyptus trees. He and our young male Rapa Nui helper got out of the truck, grabbed a chainsaw from the back, and waded into the bushes to cut firewood. It turned out that we were going to have a feast of fresh fish for lunch. We worked all morning and then came back to where the trucks were parked for lunch. There was a good fire going, and the fish were laid out on a large wire grill. Then some very thick and narrow bacon was laid on the grill. After that came little bananas. Then the fish had lemon squeezed over them. We began with finger food, little pieces of that bacon, cut on a board—wonderful. When the

Eating fish fresh off the grill in the field (courtesy Louise Jones-Takata).

fish was done, we each picked up a lettuce leaf for a plate and a plastic fork, and dug into the tender fish as someone peeled back the skin. It was delicious. Our driver spoke a steady stream of his native Rapa Nui with our helper on the drive, but his English was American, and his Chevy pickup sported California license plates. Turns out, he had a business in Long Beach, California.

Louise Jones-Takata appearing to kiss a *maoi* at Rano Raraku, the place in Rapa Nui National Park where the *maoi* were crafted (courtesy Ellen West-brook).

We didn't work all the time. One night we attended folk-dance entertainment. On the weekend, we toured the island and saw *maoi* in parks. On Sunday, we went to Mass at the Catholic Church, the Rapa Nui Mass. The place was packed. Fortunately for the old ladies who hobbled in late, Rapa Nui culture has a way of providing. A woman would get herself to the end of a pew and stand there. If no one got up or the whole group didn't scooch down to make room for her, she issued a glare that apparently could penetrate the back of a head, because soon someone would look around, fairly jump to his feet and leave. Then, like some manner of royalty, she would deign to sit down with those remaining. Yet another power *pani* in action.

One morning before breakfast, Ellen and I took a walk down the dirt road beside the place where we were staying. We ambled along between fields of crops and gardens and then realized the road dwindled and became someone's driveway, so we turned around and headed

Proof I went there (courtesy Ellen Westbrook).

The *maoi* at Anakena, a white coral sand beach in the Rapa Nui National Park (courtesy Louise Jones-Takata).

back. When we returned to the hotel, the rest of the group was sitting on the veranda, and we went to our room to get our work stuff. At some point, we heard some shouting and wondered what was going on. We noticed a police car out front. It seems a woman took offense at our walking near that house and came to complain. We had no idea what we had started until members of the team told us how she screamed and yelled and threw a clod of dirt at one of our leaders, who ignored her. The police spoke with her until she calmed down and left, and then they departed.

One of our leaders told us that mentally ill people are sent to Rapa Nui from the mainland. They may begin with caretakers and medication, but they are pretty much on their own and pretty soon stop the meds or fire the caretakers and end up roaming. That woman had caused trouble before, so they weren't concerned.

Our hosts provided lots of extra information in the form of talks

Rapa Nui church where I witnessed yet another culture's power *pani* in action (courtesy Ellen Westbrook).

by knowledgeable people. One night after dinner, we heard from a young man from a university in Arizona. He was studying spiders in the caves of Rapa Nui. We asked him about caving accidents, and he told us about an agency he had engaged that would come flying in on a private jet as soon as they had a phone call from him, should he be in trouble. I asked where the jet was based, and he confidently announced, "Boston." Call me crazy, but wouldn't hyperthermia get him before it arrived?—or maybe the rock on his chest? This is why young people do this work. They are still immortal.

Another day we went to a local art gallery and heard from an expert from the University of California. She had written a book based on her years of work on the island. Another night we listened to the woman we all knew from the gas station. Yes, the gas station happened to have a very respectable selection of wines for sale, and we often stopped to stock up. It was impossible to miss the fact that a woman who worked there spoke perfect American English. As it turns out, her grandfather was in the first Thor Heyerdahl expedition. As a scientist, he made numerous trips to the island, and, wouldn't you know it, when his daughter accompanied him on a trip, she met a Rapa Nui native, fell in love and married him. Our guest was their daughter.

People from all over the world cross paths on Rapa Nui, but it is distinctly itself. As on a lot of Polynesian islands, people travel on motor scooters—with the entire family crammed aboard—and men proudly wear their long raven black hair in a bun when not dancing in a ceremony. But most striking of all, once the plane leaves the island, you are on your own. We learned this well when one of our leaders developed an infection in her tooth. There is one dentist on the island, and there is one small hospital; this requires a great deal of waiting. In the end, she suffered several days and then boarded a plane for the mainland to see a doctor in Santiago. We all went to the airport to hug her and wish her well, then drove around to the chain-link fence at the edge of the runway and waved goodbye again as she boarded the plane—as if she was some rock star, not a woman so miserable she could barely speak.

Too soon, we were packed and heading for that airport ourselves. And this is the second thing that lets you know you are very far from everywhere else—there are no planes at the airport, until that one you are going to board or meet comes in. There is the occasional private jet: John Travolta stopped for gas once in his 747, but that's it.

We checked our luggage, got our boarding passes, and then we all piled back into the truck and went sightseeing one last time until we actually saw the plane in the sky. Then it was a slow moseying back to the airport, where we were each given a traditional feather and shell necklace and a warm hug good-bye.

Ellen and I had booked a small apartment in downtown Santiago for a post-project look-see. We spent three nights there and the days sightseeing. We went to all the museums we could handle and also were taken to lunch and a driving tour by some friends of Ellen's who insisted we contact them. Outside the largest Catholic Church in the city, we enjoyed a free concert and watched a man dressed as a miner and painted in copper colors stand like a statue. It's a beautiful city, and there was a lot to see, but I really preferred Rapa Nui—that isolation out there in the ocean where people mingle with free-range chickens, dogs, and horses. And I was really glad I had finally been fitted with hearing aids so I could appreciate both the pounding of the Pacific and the tiny cheeps of the courtyard chicks.

12

Cuba,
Ninety Miles
and a World Away—
Age 69 (2012)

A lot had happened between Rapa Nui and Cuba. Wally and I had bought a house in Florida, thinking we'd be snowbirds, and within a year decided to move there. In the midst of the chaos, my slowly degenerating vertebrae finally took me out of commission. I could not drive for months and found it difficult to walk and sit as well. When I recovered and thought about traveling, my main requirement was something not far away. From Florida, that's Cuba.

The first official Cuban I saw after getting through the locked door at the José Martí Airport in Havana was a security guard—a young woman in a khaki uniform that included a short, tight skirt, black lace stockings with roses worked into the design, and heels. Then I realized, of course, I was back in Latin America, where women are women and every outfit, can be, and often is, well, sexy, regardless of the regime. This encounter was the first little turn in what would be a head-spinning week of changing perspectives.

When I set out for Cuba, I wondered, was the place really littered with fifties-era American cars? This trip was classified as a people-to-people tour, and I had many questions. What would I learn about relations between my country and Cuba? Why were so many passengers on my flight from Miami stuffing bicycle tires into the overhead bins? Would people still be wearing fatigues? Would there be free-range chickens on the tour bus? I sincerely hoped not on the last.

Off we went to our hotel and lunch. Usually, Global Volunteers trips don't include alcohol, so I was surprised when a waitress brought each of us what seemed to be a *mojito*. Then she came around with a bottle of rum and poured, making it so. It was delicious. I don't like *mojitos* at home, nor do I drink at lunch, but when in Havana, the rules change.

We spent our first three nights at the National Hotel in downtown Havana, a splendid thirties-era building. The approach boasted towering palms, flowerbeds, and rows of fifties-era American cars waiting for tourists to ride in them. Languages from many countries created a sort of acoustical cloud of Babel in the lobby. My room was high ceilinged, with windows shrouded in enough drapery to wrap two or three Soviet tanks. The air conditioning sounded like a semi idling just above the ceiling over my bed. Elegant but antiquated. The electrical system, and that in all other rooms in which I stayed, was, let's say—creative. To complicate matters, the hotel was wired with both 110 and 220. It paid to crawl under the settee with a flashlight and check the labeling on the outlets before charging any electronics, as some of our group discovered the hard, but fast, way.

In the lobby, I changed money, handing over my U.S. dollars and receiving CUCs, or convertible Cuban pesos. These are usually worth one U.S. dollar and are used by tourists and officially only exchangeable within the country. Cubans are paid in Cuban pesos, worth much less. I then chose to ramble out the back of the hotel, which opened onto lawns, terraces and a swimming pool. The edge looked out over the *malecón*, a broad walkway, roadway and seawall stretching four miles along the coast.

That night, we walked to dinner at a restaurant on the top floor of a nearby building. Streetlights, when they existed, didn't give out much light. People were apparently heading to the parties that we could hear and glimpse on apartment balconies. At our destination, we boarded the weight-challenged elevator in groups of ten, as instructed. Thirty-three floors would be a long way to drop. Unlike in the paranoid U.S., the huge windows in the restaurant opened so we could conveniently lean out and take photos of the city at night far below and enjoy the early evening rain as it wafted over our food. We were entertained by two women—one playing a keyboard and the other a violin—who sang songs from the fifties. That was the first night we heard "Guantanamera," a love song about a woman from Guantanamo. When they took a break, the musicians came around and sold us CDs of their music or asked for donations. This would happen every time musicians entertained us. We had been advised earlier on how much to tip, including the ladies in the restrooms who collected a dime or so for the tiny portion of toilet paper they gave us. As in other countries south of our border, toilet paper is not flushed but deposited in a conveniently located waste can next to each toilet. That's all I'll say on that topic. If you go there, get used to it.

On Sunday, we had plenty of time for breakfast, which turned out to be buffet style and enormous. There were eggs cooked any way you liked, pancakes being flipped, a man cutting fresh fruit, tables piled high with pastries, something called Ohio sausage, which was spicy and nothing like I can imagine anyone in Ohio eating. There were vegetables and rice, just about everything except pizza and soft-serve ice cream. But, the best by far was the Cuban coffee—oh my.

After breakfast, we boarded the tour bus, which was made in China; it was shiny, new, comfortable, and poultry free. Our first destination was Ernest Hemingway's home, a beautiful place with expansive grounds, a tower, a pool, and his boat, the Pilar, in dry dock. The house is filled with his things—books, African hunting trophies, desks, and clothes. One of the women in our group used to go to Cuba when she was a child to visit relatives. She tried to give an American dollar to a Cuban woman working in the tower. The woman could not take it. She had no way of spending it. She did accept one CUC, however, worth about 87 cents at that time.

On our way back to the bus, we stopped at a tiny palm-thatched bar. One man was whacking the green husks off coconuts with a machete. Others were pressing sugar cane and collecting the juice in a pitcher. All this went to the bartender, who had a supply of fresh pineapple, oranges, lemons and who knows what else. As it turns out, we were being offered free drinks again. I looked at my watch—not yet noon. I looked at the fruit and the rum. Yes, why not?

Lunch was at a government-run restaurant where we were offered wine or beer. I had to pass or nap the afternoon away. This restaurant had a big sign in the entry about the Cuban Five, five heroes currently

Hemingway's closet, with lots of shoes and boots and what looks like a military jacket. We could only look into the interior from the outside of the house.

being held captive in the United States. In Miami, they are called spies—another perspective.

From there, it was down to old Havana to join Cubans who wanted to meet with us and practice their English. I went with two women from our group and a Cuban named Samuel, an unemployed electrician. He told us he could work all day and earn fifty-five cents, so the 87 cents that went to the woman in the tower was not as insignificant as I had thought. It is true that each Cuban has a ration book and goes to a state store to get basic food items, but only if they are available. Cubans also have free health care, from the sniffles to the most complicated surgery. Their medical system seems to be well regarded internationally. Education is free through university levels.

But 50 cents a day? You should have heard how he said it. Still, Cubans were hopeful about changes to their system because they had experienced some in the last few years. They could now own property, if they could get the money. Many Cubans have families in the U.S. who send them money. These funds are referred to as allotments. The money must come electronically, and that means, like their version of the Internet, it is monitored and controlled by the government.

We walked with Samuel back to meet the others in the restored area of downtown Havana. The buildings are heavy colonial concoctions of decoration, columns, balconies, and terraces. A block or two away is the same architecture, but it is falling down on people's heads. Children were running and playing with a toy, which soared into the air like a lighted rocket and then tumbled back to earth. They were launched by rubber bands. These turned out to be the only toys I would see on this trip.

Regular cars belonging to those who could afford them.

Santería, like *candomblé* in Brazil, is an African-based religion and has a strong presence on the island. I recognized the women followers, all in white and puffing those tar-black cigars.

When we reached a restaurant where we had dinner, we were offered chicken, fish, or beef. Most Cubans see little fish or beef. Our guide told us cow owners have to have permission to kill a cow. If permission is granted, someone with a license to own a gun comes and does the deed. Consequently, some cows get hit by buses. In any case, they are old dairy cows, and I knew the meat would be tough. It was, but it was also flavorful. I dined with an American couple from our group that produces 6,000 hogs a year on their farm back home; now, there's a perspective.

On Monday, we headed out for a meeting with people from the Cuban Council of Churches. I went off on a short trip to la-la land during the first part, but then, the speaker's words caught my interest. The council was formed in 1941 and includes a mix of churches, Presbyterian, Greek Orthodox, Church of Christ, etc. The Catholics are not part of the council, but Catholicism is alive and well, or the Pope would not have visited that very year.

The organization works on everything from sustainable development to emergency response and helping senior citizens and people with substance-abuse problems. Their work was impressive, especially considering that religion had been banned in 1969 and that the ban had lasted nearly three decades. Our guide told us that the generation that grew up in that period thinks Christmas trees, which are re-emerging, are as pretty and meaningless as disco balls.

Having arrived in this country shortly after Hurricane Sandy hit Cuba and the U.S., it was interesting to hear some of the differences in people's situations. About 10,000 people lost their roofs in parts of Cuba hit by the storm. One of the problems is the use of the cheapest roofing material, corrugated metal—which I watched a man cut vertically using a machete and a small sledgehammer. It was slow going. They have an emergency response system, and people are evacuated. I had the impression that, unlike in the U.S., if you are told to leave, you evacuate, one way or another.

At a typical church-picnic-style lunch with members of the council and our conversation partners from the previous day, I met a young man who badly wanted to go to North Dakota. This was puzzling. He said his neighbor had been there and told him how beautiful it was. A couple of us told him how cold it got there, and he shrugged it off, never having been away from Cuba where it rarely dips as low as freezing in winter. He had no concept of the kind of cold that freezes your nose hairs stiff. When I mentioned it was empty, I got his attention. I

Cuba's capitol building. Look familiar? It's modeled after the U.S. Capitol.

described being able to drive for hours between towns and seeing no one. That gave him pause, but he was still in love with the notion of North Dakota, even though we suggested something more moderate, like Kentucky.

From there, we went to the University of Havana's Center for Hemispheric and U.S. Studies. There, Olga Rosa Gonzalez Martin addressed "The Conflict Between Cuba and the US: Its Current State." She was articulate and well educated. She had traveled abroad but had no interest in leaving Cuba, as it is her home, and she wants to help improve it. Her talk was full of interesting material, starting with the fact that our Founding Fathers considered Cuba part of the U.S. because, according to them, the island was made from the sand that flowed down the Mississippi River. Maybe that's why one of them later thought that islands could capsize. President Thomas Jefferson considered possessing Cuba for strategic reasons and sent secret agents to the island to negotiate with Cuban Governor Salvador José de Muro y Salazar, 2nd Marquis of Someruelos. Which makes me wonder, was Jefferson puffing Cuban cigars at Monticello and the White House? Has nothing changed?

When John Quincy Adams was Secretary of State, he came up with what is often referred to as the Ripe Fruit Theory. Basically, the U.S. is big; Cuba is small and nearby. The United States is the tree, and Cuba is the fruit. According to Mr. Adams, we needed to make sure that when Spain no longer ruled the island, we gained control to protect ourselves from the next ruler to scoop her up—like ripe, fallen fruit. He went on to describe Cuba as "incapable."

Let me tell you, that kind of talk is exceedingly annoying to the Cubans. The fact that Castro was not at the table with President Kennedy and Russia's Nikita Khrushchev during the Cuban Missile Crisis negotiations still stings. In October of 1962, one of our spy planes photographed missile sites in Cuba. Khrushchev had reached an agreement with Fidel Castro for their presence in Cuba after the U.S. made a failed attempt to invade Cuba at the Bay of Pigs. It was possible, some said probable, that nuclear war would erupt. After several days of high tension, Kennedy and Khrushchev reached an agreement. Russia would remove missiles from Cuba, and America would remove hers from Turkey. No one asked Fidel Castro for his opinion.

It had been a long time since I had sat in a classroom and heard the words "Monroe Doctrine." The Bay of Pigs and the Cuban Missile Crisis occurred when I was in college and totally absorbed in my own little world. I vaguely remembered the boat people, but I didn't recall the "Wet Foot, Dry Foot" policy. As for restrictions on travel and remittances, I was not aware of which of our presidents did what in terms of what impacted Cubans' lives. It was overwhelming.

Back at the hotel, before dinner, I sat beneath sea grape trees at a table and sipped a daiquiri. My view included the lawn, tropical landscaping, and beyond, as well as the crashing waves of the Florida Straits. Just ahead of me, but unseen, was a bunker containing historic and disabled cannon aimed toward, well, my new home, Florida. Talk about perspectives....

That night, I went to the hotel business office to use a computer to e-mail Wally and check my messages. It cost me five CUCs, a little over four dollars U.S., and it took about fifteen minutes. If my math is correct, that would be about eight days' salary for Samuel. It was also a high price to pay for so little computer time, compared with other countries I'd visited.

On Tuesday morning, we boarded the bus and headed for the city of Ciego de Avila in the center of the country, the capital of a province having the same name. It was a long ride. At our first rest stop, we played guinea pig roulette. A bunch of us stuffed paper CUCs into the tops of little wooden houses on a round table. A guinea pig was placed on a platform covered with a little house and gently spun. Then it was let loose to find a treat hidden in one of the houses. The winner was the person who had stuck his money into the house containing the treat. The prize was a bottle of rum. I did not win.

We stopped next in Santa Clara at the Ernesto "Che" Guevara mausoleum, museum and monument. The section where Che and his men are buried is beautifully designed and partially underground. Light from candles and the sun, streaming through openings in the ceiling, creates a quiet and reverential feeling. There are fresh flowers and an eternal flame. Any American my age knows the iconic photos of Che Guevara, the handsome sidekick of Fidel Castro. In photos, he is usually seen wearing a beret and often smoking a cigar. I must say, if the cigars are as good as the coffee and the rum, I'd smoke them, too. In the museum, we saw images of Che and other revolutionaries, always smoking something, and a couple of Che with a golf club in hand—one as a child in Argentina, with a small putter, and another goofing around with the other rebels in fatigues. It was a beautiful monument, and the statue in front was the usual Soviet super-size. He is a Cuban hero and has become the icon of revolutionary causes around the world. Our tour guide told us a great deal about him on our bus ride, including the fact that he was killed by the CIA, something I did remember. I considered her perspective. Her country's hero was murdered. My country hunted him down in Bolivia and shot him. He was a freedom fighter. Americans revere freedom unless those fighters are also Marxists.

We passed huge fields of sugar cane and small farms with what would be considered antique tractors back home. In the afternoon, we arrived at our Soviet-era hotel. When the Soviet Union was helping support Cuba, they came in ready to make progress in a hurry. That meant setting up concrete factories that could turn out huge slabs of building parts—the ubiquitous block look seen in Eastern Europe and other areas where they had influence. The Hotel Ciego de Avila was one of these constructions. It was brightly painted, and the architecture was quite interesting and open, sort of 1950s modern. I entered my room and realized all the design was on the outside. The drapes, while clean, were that typical beige and brown so chic when Howdy Doody was a star. Walls were unadorned blah, and the furniture was made of heavy plywood painted a sticky looking brown. The extra blanket was downright scary, a fright I got over when it got cold that night. The bathroom was nicely redone, except for the hot water, which was missing the first night. Only the balcony was brightly painted, yellow and green.

After dinner with the usual libations of rum, most of us got on a sort of clown train and were taken downtown to a club—concrete room with musicians and amps, small tables—and, God help us, more free drinks. The trainload of little cars, pulled by some gas engine contraption, pulled away from the restaurant in the dark, with all of us quite merry. At the club, we were hosted by—are you ready for this?— the Baptists, who were gettin' down in a big way. We were pulled to our feet and learned to dance and clap and have a deafening good time.

The next day was jam-packed and started with the laying of

flowers at the feet of a statue of José Martí in José Martí Square. José Julián Martí y Pérez was born January 28, 1853, in Havana and died May 19, 1895, in Dos Ríos, Cuba, in battle. He was a poet and an essayist and lived for a while in New York, as well as other countries. His fight for Cuba's liberation from Spain caused him to seek refuge in different countries through the years. Some of his work encouraged Latin American countries to learn from the United States while forming their own ways of governing. The song "Guantanamera" was taken from his poetry and became popular in other parts of the world when Pete Seeger taught it to us.

After the guide told us about this leader, we went to a museum, where we were treated to a terrific dance performance based on traditional Cuban dances. Back on the bus and lunch at a lake—curiously devoid of pleasure boats. There seemed to be no toys in Cuba. I didn't see any littering backyards or kids playing with them on the street. People riding motorcycles were obviously going somewhere, not just out for a spin. You can tell. It's like knowing when a person is walking for exercise and when they are trying to get somewhere. This made me think the people I saw fishing were not practicing catch and release; they were practicing catch and eat.

Our next stop was a renovated theater where we learned what the acting troupe does for communities in the area, watched a performance, got involved in one ourselves, and had a discussion with members of the troupe. They don't just entertain: they add education about preventing sexually transmitted diseases and about seeking help for domestic violence, for instance. We met up with the same people at dinner that night.

At my table, we talked with a young man who was studying English and French at university and had already done his required military service, which he disliked. We asked what his job had been in the military, and he said he had been a guard. When asked what he guarded, he gave us a puzzled look and simply said, "Cuba." End of discussion. He seemed hopeful about coming changes that will be good for his country, mentioning the lifting of travel restrictions for Cubans that was scheduled to begin January 14, 2013. He was not the first Cuban to mention this to us. I wondered what his perspective was about repatriation.

As I was waiting to leave the restaurant, a man who may have been the owner or manager asked me about my meal. We talked more, and he said he thought it was important for Cuba to open and asked if I would come back. I told him I thought people like us—who wanted to come here—would go home and share our experiences with people we knew—a grass-roots level of sharing that would surely help. I asked if he had been to the United States. He had not, but he had been out of the country, to Africa. He said he had been a young soldier in Angola and Ethiopia, two years each. He said he had been only 20 years old and added that he wanted no more war, in a way that indicated he had seen things he wanted to forget, but could not. I wanted to talk more but had to board the bus. My head was spinning with these experiences. I was a newlywed when American men were flying off to the war in Vietnam. My high school students were being whisked out of my classroom to serve. Those who came back and dropped by to visit had clearly become men. I also remember a veteran of that war mentioning his worst interrogator, when he was captured, was a Cuban.

The next day we saw several different parts of Ciego de Avila. There were the streets clogged with bicycles—remember the bicycle tires stuffed into the bins on the plane? Plenty of bikes, few parts. There were also pedicabs, the ever-present representatives of 1950s Detroit, as well as our modern bus with the Chinese lettering on the outside, the occasional horse, and a tractor or two. Private shops were open along these streets. When given permission to exercise a little free enterprise, the Cubans literally opened their doors. Either the front door or a window in a front room would be open to the street and some goods offered for sale. At one, you could buy pastries or a sandwich. At another, what looked like used women's clothing was displayed. An official state store, where Cubans shopped with their ration books, looked poor in everything, save cigarettes.

Then, we turned the corner and entered a different world, one we were all familiar with, a gentrified pedestrian mall. New paving, lighting, flowers and fountains and modern shops with big glass doors. On that street, we peered into the same size small shops as those we had just seen lurking at the edges of private living rooms. These seemed well stocked with new merchandise. We visited a bookstore, an art gal-

Store in someone's home. Dogs welcome. The sign says, "Open."

lery, and a craft gallery. These fine stores were all government-owned, as were the few department-style stores we had glimpsed in Havana.

After our tour, we met with the dancing Baptists again. Their minister was our host in this part of the trip, and he was a very down-to-earth fellow. He had arranged for us to go to the church and meet with some senior citizens. He acted as a translator, and the discussion was lively. We were served Russian tea, as in—it came from Russia. These people remembered the Cuban Missile Crisis and how they were ready to defend themselves from whatever happened. "We have lived our whole life in crisis," one said. When asked what they wanted, they said they wanted the embargo lifted, for the sake of their children and grandchildren, and to live in peace. They also referred

The same store from across street. All the houses seemed very dark inside, as though they were careful with their electricity, or it wasn't on at all.

to the embargo as a blockade. They said an embargo is between two countries, but some countries trading with the U.S. were fined if they also traded with Cuba: that made it a blockade.

The discussion became more complicated when someone said Cubans in Miami did not want the embargo lifted until the regime changed. There was a fog of viewpoints. One Cuban man made an emotional plea, asking us if President Obama, when he was helping his daughters with their homework, explained why the U.S. wouldn't let Cuban children with cancer have the medicine they need. Back and forth we went, engaged, but seemingly without rancor.

Then one of our group stood up and told a story about working with a Chinese nationalist in the U.S. who did not want to return home when it was time. The Chinese man was highly educated and would have a good job in China. When asked why he didn't want to go back, the man said because in the U.S., he was free—and our orator paused, raised his fist and said, "free," again as if he had an American flag in his hand.

Everyone got quiet. We had accidentally offended our hosts. Finally, a Cuban woman raised her hand and said she was free. She didn't

Food for sale from someone's home. Again, a dark interior.

need to leave her country to be free. Another gave the example of needing to walk alone down a city street to obtain medicine at three in the morning and having no concern for her safety. The Cuban group leader talked about his experiences in the U.S. and how he felt safer from physical attack in Cuba.

Then to lighten the mood, he told a joke. It seems Raul Castro and Barack Obama had a secret meeting. All went well, and then at the end, Raul asked, "When are you going to give us back Guantanamo?"

Official store with very little in it that we could see.

Obama asked in return, "When are you going to give us back Miami?"

Since it was our Thanksgiving, we stood, and someone said a prayer of thanks. Then we sang "Guantanamera" together.

There was hugging and picture-taking as we slowly headed out. That afternoon we returned to Havana and the National Hotel. As a surprise, that night we dined on turkey in the finest restaurant in the hotel. Waiters in regalia brought us wine, and a woman played a grand piano about a football field away, at the other end of the room. I couldn't help but think of my mother-in-law, who sometimes traveled by ship from Mexico to New York in the thirties. She talked of packing evening gowns and dancing in Havana, where the ship stopped for a few nights. Perhaps she had swept around that very room. It was a pleasant holiday thought. To top it off, the man who won the bottle of rum playing Guinea pig roulette shared it with us.

On Friday, I awoke with "Guantanamera" wearing a deep groove in my brain. After breakfast, it was off to a rum factory, where we learned that the stuff is aged in barrels made of white oak from Tennessee—via Canada. Then we toured downtown and the capitol building and went on to the Museum of the Revolution, which was in the building that used to be the Presidential Palace back in Batista's day. Inside, except for the holes made in the marble by high caliber weapons, the palace looked like Versailles. Tiffany & Co. designed the opulent interior.

Upstairs, we saw a temporary art show based on the Cuban Five's being held in Miami. I knew some of the America-bashing was beginning to disturb some members of our group, but they were never poor guests and did not mention it in front of Cubans. The most in-your-face statement was down a hallway where there were huge cutout caricatures of Fulgencio Batista (in military uniform), Ronald Reagan (as a cowboy), George Bush, Sr. (in a sort of Roman soldier outfit), and George W. Bush (wearing a Nazi helmet and reading a book upside down). They were called "cretins" and thanked in several languages for their help with the Revolution.

After lunch and a saunter through the second-hand bookstalls in the square, we went to the U.S. Interests Section. The section was the nearest thing to an embassy we had in Cuba at the time. Our tour guide, who got us into every place we went, had to stay on the bus as we crossed the street, two by two, when given the signal by a guard. We showed our passports to a woman high up in an armored station. Then we passed through a screening room and up a hill to another security checkpoint. There we surrendered our passports to a U.S. Marine who was seated behind thick bulletproof glass. Then we got our badges and went to a briefing room. In a few minutes, a young diplomat, in tie and shirtsleeves, came in—red Solo cup in hand. It was time for the official American perspective.

His approach was not about what the U.S. was going to do for or about Cuba; it was about where the Cuban government was going to take Cuba next. He confirmed everything we had already gleaned by meeting with Cubans and listening to our guide—average income was about $20 a month, and health, housing and education were taken care of, but it wasn't enough. The government had allowed limited private-sector enterprise.

The young diplomat also said that the Cuban Five were what was left of a fourteen-person group that had been arrested—and that one of the Five had been released. According to him, the government puts up the signs about the Cuban Five, and that concern is not spontaneous from the people. He also talked about the American, Alan Gross, who was being held in Cuba at that time and added that Cuba had a lot of "cold war baggage." Police were still picking up people for questioning. One of the Cubans in our conversation group said that, after we left her, she was questioned by the police because she had talked with tourists. The Internet Cubans could access was restricted by the government.

However, the diplomat also said that people overall were more forthcoming than they used to be and not as cautious about what they said. In his 15 years as a diplomat, he told us, he had never served in a place where the U.S. was so important to the people and so low on U.S. radar. That perspective is not one that can come easily to many Cubans like our friends Samuel and the would-be North Dakota resident, who had never left the island— and whose information about the outside world is filtered. Their perspectives are controlled.

That was our last day. We had a surprise that night—we got to ride around Havana in those beautiful old convertibles on our way to dinner. I chose a cherry red 1958 Chevy with a white interior and fake roses on the dash. Our drivers, who owned the cars, drove slowly and laced the night air with a shrill bouquet of horn tunes. Some of us women climbed up on the back seats and waved like beauty queens— thank goodness it was dark. Three of the men in the group piled into one car and seemed transported back in time. For them, it must have been a jumble of memories: engines, Simonizing, laying rubber and looking for cops, girls with skirts as big as parachutes snuggled next to them. Such a nice ride.

I had chosen Cuba as a traveling trial to find out if flying would be bad for my back. There were times riding in a car when I had to ward off jarring from a bumpy road by holding myself up with my hands. In a plane, you can't see bumps coming and can be taken by surprise. It turned out to be fine, and I felt like I had visited some long-hidden neighbors. It also turned out to be more fascinating than I ever imagined.

13

Colorado,
Digging in the Dirt—
Age 74 (2017)

Two years after the Cuba adventure, I considered doing an Earthwatch project in the U.S. I had never done one in-country before. I hadn't had any more back attacks and managed to find a really lightweight carryon that was going to be my luggage for the weeklong program. The archaeology I had done in Armenia—recording the measurements of endangered architecture—and the work done in Rapa Nui, mapping ancient garden sites, was nothing like the stereotypical dig I had in mind. Those projects and work taught me more about the breadth of the academic field of archaeology, but I wanted to play at being Indiana Jones instead. I didn't have an old, banged-up fedora, but I did have work gloves, boots and a healthy respect for snakes.

The project was at Crow Canyon Archaeological Center in Cortez, Colorado, in the southwestern part of the state, not far from Mesa Verde National Park. We would stay in hogans—round log structures, patterned after the Navajo houses of old—that looked ever-so-charming on the website.

Wally and I had celebrated our 50th wedding anniversary in Santa Fe the year before, and I found I liked getting back to the West and its mountains. That was another reason I thought I would like this trip. I had even talked Ellen into joining me and into adding a little road trip through the area afterward. We had booked a nice condo in ski country and planned to rent a car. Sort of Thelma and Louise without the shooting and certainly without the ending. Well, it turned out there was drama but no ending at all. Ellen had to cancel because a hurricane

Some of the hogans in which we stayed (courtesy Mary Rowe, Expedition Advisor, Earthwatch).

came along, and the mahogany tree next to her house dropped a limb on her roof large enough to require a crane to remove it.

I canceled the condo and the car, Ellen stayed home to take care of matters, and I set off for Colorado. The first leg of the trip was the usual airport sights and sounds. Then, in the waiting area for the next leg to Durango, which would be on a smaller plane, I saw a different sort of passenger. Friends and family had been texting me about marijuana shops at the airport. No, there were none, but a waiting passenger, a youngish man who looked like he may have come out of the mountains with a pack mule, reacted to an ongoing audible and annoying electronic signal by asking loudly, "Does anyone else hear that?" Then he got up and left. Hmm, I thought, I think I'm heading for the far outback, or maybe he's tripping. Anyway, the clothes on the passengers were different, all hiking or cowboy boots, heavy vests and beardy—if you were of the Y-chromosome persuasion. Off I went with a pack of possible cowpunchers.

13. Colorado, Digging in the Dirt

After we were collected at the Durango Airport, we boarded a van and headed off on a long drive—an hour or more—to our destination. Passing through the last town of sorts before Crow Canyon, I could see we were indeed out in the country. The campus was both rustic and charming, and we headed directly to our hogans, which were connected by sidewalks. The view was spectacular with the Rockies lightly dusted with snow at the top. Each hut contained enough beds for six, four singles and a bunk, but we were few enough of us that there were only two people in each. Nearby, there was a super-hogan with toilets and showers. We had been warned that at an altitude of 6,200 feet, people from lower levels (sea level, in my case) might have difficulty with the changes. I was fine. We settled in and then headed for the cafeteria for our first dinner. The small kitchen staff seemed to employ local natives, and the food was plentiful. Seconds were available, but only after everyone had been served once. And they knew if you came back too soon and sent you away. Sometimes we shared with visiting school children, who were there to learn about archaeology and about not busting food lines.

After a short break, we jumped right in with our first lecture. Dr. Susan Ryan, the director of archaeology at the center, was the Principal Investigator and our boss. You might think that working all day and listening to lectures at night was a bit much, but it is not when it is fascinating. I was a blank slate and welcomed every word Susan chalked onto me, starting with basic terminology—broken pottery parts are "sherds" not shards, and broken glass parts are "shards," not smashed glass. Then we moved on to difficult ideas, such as how the transition from hunting-and-gathering to agriculture might have happened. Now that's a question I never thought about and instantly found compelling.

That night, my roommate and I made our beds and climbed in. It was cold. There was a heater above a window, and the heat went straight up to the conical ceiling. Our hogan was reminiscent of the South African *rondavel* but without the hot water bottle. I piled on the extra bedding, which consisted of cotton coverlets. Good thing I had brought the same wool hoodie and socks I took on almost every trip. Still chilly.

Our training began the next day. We visited the site in the morning and the lab in the afternoon. We would be doing everything. We would be focusing on parts of a great house in the area. From the project briefing, I learned that the overall goals included assessing the identity of ancient migrants by evaluating architectural production and the presence of non-local artifacts. The archaeologists also wanted to find out how the great houses related to each other. In addition, they wanted to look at how growing populations affected the environment, at how a 50-year drought (between 1130 and 1180 CE) affected the availability of resources, and at how the residents adapted to a changing climate.

The dig site at an ancestral pueblo settlement was in an area with a house and a nonworking automotive shop/garage. Crow Canyon was able to raise enough funds to buy the place when it went on the market. When it was private property, the owners had mined the area for artifacts to sell. They actually brought in bulldozers and wrecked areas. That's because it is legal to keep or sell artifacts found on your own property, except for human remains. It seems scandalous now, but we were reminded that some early archaeologists were little more than grave robbers. That's why Western museums are now considering returning treasures to the countries in which they were found.

In 1891, Gustaf Nordenskiöld came to the Mesa Verde area from Sweden. As a scientist, he was very helpful in the work at Mesa Verde, where he excavated ruins and surveyed sites. As a foreigner, he was inadvertently helpful in getting the U.S. Antiquities Act in place as well. If Nordenskiöld hadn't been an outsider, the locals might not have had him arrested when his boxcars loaded with artifacts reached Durango. Concern over others having what seemed to belong to them led to unrest that eventually achieved the Antiquities Act and Mesa Verde National Park status. Because there was no law against removing artifacts then, after some delay, the treasure left Colorado and went to Europe.

Even though the previous owners had ransacked the place where we were working, the site was still littered with artifacts. Just walking from the parking area to the garage, we spotted painted sherds all over the place, and we barely knew what we were doing. We were told not to pick them up, but to leave them where they lay, just like the basalt tool found on Rapa Nui. I so wanted to stuff those things into my pockets the way we did when I was a kid at the Petrified Forest before the pebble police showed up.

We saw the shallow pits where we would work and learned how

to use the sieve hanging from a tripod. Susan explained how to sort the different sizes and kinds of finds—pottery, lithics (chipped stone), ground stone, animal bone, and other forms of material culture—and which bags to use to store them. The plots were measured into grids and levels, and the work recorded accordingly. We worked in these areas in the mornings. The mind was willing, but the knees weren't too happy to be getting up and down and kneeling—on a gardening pad—but kneeling.

The sieve to which we hauled our dug-up earth and strained it for finds.

The first question out of anyone who finds out you went on a dig is, "Did you find anything?" Well, sure, I found a lot of unremarkable little pieces of pottery, stone tool parts, all the stuff we were taught to recognize. But, I know the person asking wants to know if I found treasure, a skull, a long-lost code. The answer is, "Almost." There was a conical pile of sifted dirt next to the area where I was digging with a partner. We walked past that pile every time we took a bucket of dirt to the sieve and every time we came back. I noticed a perfectly round pink bead on that pile and thought—plastic, and I kept on going. Then on one trip, my partner, an actual archaeologist, spotted it and picked it up. It was indeed an ancient bead. Just a few feet away, another volunteer found a perfect tiny arrowhead. So, the best answer is "almost."

Lunch was packed in a cooler that we would bring with us, and we used the garage with its picnic tables as a place to eat the sandwiches, fruit and snacks we prepared for ourselves. After lunch, we headed back to the campus for our tour of the lab. That's where the bags of

Left: Tiny arrowhead probably used for hunting small birds. This was found in the section next to the one where I was working. *Right:* Small bead found in the sieve siftings. Can you imagine making this by hand with the most primitive of tools?

sherds, etc., were washed, sorted again, weighed, measured, recorded and stored. Playing in the water looked like the most fun as the designs on the sherds were revealed and "oohed" and "aahed" over. After dinner, we had another lecture.

It may have been on this trip that I realized how much I loved the learning on this kind of travel. Or maybe it was in Cuba when I realized that. But Cuba was a different kind of learning. It was about the recent past and the present. At these ruins, my mind went back in time, and I imagined life in this enormous settlement of interconnecting buildings and rooms. The earth was the same. The people who lived here a thousand years ago and left the things we were finding experienced the same chill at night, the same wet in the rain and dust in the wind. As I learned more and more about these ancient people, I could imagine life stripped to their bare but rich existence, collecting food and water, making pots and decorating them with brushes made of yucca fiber. As an artist who has dabbled in weaving and basket making, I could see how easily a pattern could evolve in the necessary grid of basket engineering.

The painting on the pots seemed to echo the same patterns before they diverged into freer forms no longer constrained by the mathematical weaving process. When I held a large potsherd from the Anasazi Heritage Center collection on my lap, I felt a leap through space and time. The strokes could have been made with a broad felt-tip marker or a modern brush. I had seen the same shapes and marks in paintings by artists across a wide spectrum of cultures—in Japanese calligraphy and even in my own sketchbooks. Here was proof of the ancient aphorism by Hippocrates, "*Ars longa, vita brevis.*" Art is long; life is short. It was a connection I never dreamed of experiencing, and I did my best to hang onto it.

An example of the tremendousness of the population now gone can be found in the remains of the best-known great house, Pueblo Bonito, in Chaco Canyon in northwest New Mexico. Built between 800 and 1140 CE, this construction had between 600 and 800 rooms and was five stories high. There was a built-in ventilation system that brought fresh air to all the interior rooms. Collectively, these great houses were the densest concentration of the largest buildings found anywhere in the ancestral pueblo world.

Years before, Wally and I had been out this way camping and had learned about the Anasazi. We were told then that the people simply disappeared, and no one knew why. In preparation for this trip, I read some recommended books and articles, and a source, now misplaced, mentioned the Anasazi hadn't disappeared at all. They were everywhere in this region. They were the Diné, or Navajo. Maybe yes, maybe no. Recent research suggests the Ancestral Puebloans (as they are now known) were not one people, so there is no direct line. In fact, the word Anasazi is out of favor as it is a Navajo word unrelated to pueblo peoples and is a veiled insult sometimes translated as "enemy ancestors." Times change; more is revealed, and we learn.

The 50-year drought had forced people from this area to go to the Chaco Canyon, but that region was also too dry to sustain them. By 1130 CE, the people had begun to migrate east, west and south.

We learned about different theories of how the New World was populated. In Alaska, I had learned of the Athabaskans, and here I discovered that those people traveled south to become the Navajo. In Rapa Nui, I learned about the population drift from Polynesia to the New World's southern hemisphere, and here I was learning of the theory known as the kelp highway. This idea suggests that early peoples lived off kelp forests in the ocean as they traveled up the coast of the Americas.

Once we learned to work in the lab, we could see the enormous amount of material that was sorted and cataloged and stored. It's physical data, carefully recorded and piled in boxes on shelves. There is another aspect of archaeology we learned about from Rebecca Simon, an archaeologist who actually owns a fedora. One of her many interests in the field is outreach, and she told us one night about a project she organized with the children in a local school who went out and investigated an old section of town and recreated part of its history with their work. When it came to what an archaeologist looks like and does, the kids were like me: they wanted a version of Indiana Jones. When Rebecca met the kids for the first time, she modeled the sun-bleached baseball cap she wears in the field, then—to cheers—she produced her fedora and planted it on her head. I wonder if someone like Rebecca had shown up at my school early on, I would have pursued a different path.

Crow Canyon does a lot of work educating those outside the field. Not only do groups of kids come through with their teachers, adults like us come through Earthwatch, and others also come and learn what we learned through research and lab programs for adults and families, teens and college students. Crow Canyon researchers also inform and consult local tribal members.

Earthwatch volunteers digging (courtesy Mary Rowe, Expedition Advisor, Earthwatch).

189

The campus, with its magnificent views of the mountains, was a lovely place to hang out when we had a little time to do it. There was a row of rocking chairs on the porch of the dining room, and we would line up there regardless of the weather to rock and enjoy. We had a couple of free evenings, one after a reception for one of the volunteers. Crow Canyon was Warren's 100th Earthwatch project. There was cake, the presentation of a golden trowel, the thanks from the President and CEO of Earthwatch, who had come from Boston for the event.

Another good place to hang was in a sort of living room in the reception area. There we drank coffee and swapped stories of other Earthwatch projects around the world. Warren was able to fill us in on details from many, maybe most of them.

Colorado wasn't that far from home as the plane flies, but my experience there, learning about the ancient pueblo peoples, made it seem like a far greater distance. There is an art term, "mark making," that refers to the basic line, dot, pattern or texture made by the hand. It is expressed in any medium. Now I have held sherds of pottery with marks made by people a thousand years ago, and if that isn't a soul souvenir, I don't know what one is.

14

Portugal, Ancient Clams, Fresh Tomatoes and a Countess— Age 75 (2018)

The Colorado archaeology trip was so interesting that I couldn't help noticing there was another opportunity in Portugal. A further draw was the focus of the study. The archaeologists were looking at the transition from the last hunter-gatherers to the first farming communities in the "Old Continent." Knowing a bit about soil from my farm days, I looked at the site in Portugal and deduced I would also be digging in softer dirt than I had experienced in Colorado. That stuff had been either hard as rock or as sticky as clay. According to the project briefing, the site in Portugal is on one of the biggest and most important shell middens in Europe. It was discovered in the late 19th century and had recently become a national monument.

On arrival in Lisbon, I realized once again how bad I am at geography. Not the navigation basics like where I am and how to get around, but the global aspect—as in, where exactly is Portugal? I had the notion that it was sort of north and west of France and north of Spain. I was so wrong, which is why the palms growing outside the airport in Lisbon surprised me. I was right, however, about the dirt being softer. The provided information taught me that the region where the Muge Shell middens are located is in a transition zone between two major ecosystems: the Atlantic (to the north) and the Mediterranean (to the south). Because of this ecosystem complexity, the region is home to a diverse range of flora and fauna. So, it wasn't just my lack of knowledge about geography: this area is a mix.

The year 2018 was the first that the Muge Shell middens project was affiliated with Earthwatch, and the organization was well organized and ready—except for our accommodations. Fortunately for us, the Countess Teresa Álvares Pereira Schönborn-Wiesentheid, CEO da Casa Cadaval and owner of the land where the shell middens are located, opened her royal home to us. The Countess runs the estate and its winery and is the latest of five generations of women to hold that position. In addition to 42 hectares of vineyards, the property also grows cork trees and produces olive oil, rice and vegetables. Casa Cadaval is one of the world's oldest breeders of Lusitano horses as well. Lusitanos are related to the Spanish Andalusians but are a separate breed, thought to be the oldest breed of horse in the world. It was wonderful to watch one of these fine animals being walked down the cobblestone streets by a rider in full non-cowboy riding gear. As for vegetables, my roommate Jane and I had a nice view of the plum tomatoes in the fields below and the huge trucks filled with them waiting to go to the processing plant. The courtyard of the palace had orange trees loaded with green fruit as well. We were 50 miles north of Lisbon in Casa Cadaval, a place that has been in the family of the Countess since 1648 and totals more than 5,400 hectares, almost 21 square miles.

We entered the gates to the outer courtyard and passed through the small orange grove to the gates of the palace itself. There we were instructed on the code to enter those gates and then the wood door. The inner courtyard was a lovely fountain-centered area with covered walkways around the perimeter. Our area was upstairs and to the left of the entrance. Rooms were high ceilinged and airy with huge windows. We were two to a room with a large bath between each. The palace had been modernized and had air conditioning, which Jane and I rarely used in our corner room with four large windows and wood shutters. We were shown the kitchen we would use to make our own breakfasts and lunches and the covered balcony where we ate outdoors. Food would show up in the kitchen, and we would prepare and eat it twice a day. Dinners were in restaurants where we enjoyed delicious stews and plenty of local wine.

14. Portugal, Clams, Tomatoes and a Countess

Courtyard at the home of the countess where we stayed (courtesy Mary Rowe, Expedition Advisor, Earthwatch).

On the first morning, we boarded the van with our bottles of water, work gloves and sun hats and headed to the excavation site just ten minutes away, in an area next to some of the vineyards. A short walk through the dry, sandy soil and we reached the tented site. The scientists let us know that previously obtained radiocarbon dates showed human occupation at this place from c. 8,000 to 7,400 years ago. With our help, the research would lead to a better understanding of the transition from Mesolithic hunter-gatherers to Neolithic farmers in that region. Again, that fascinating change led to farming and so changed our society.

As usual, we were a group with a variety of skill levels. Some had never done this, I had only done it once, and one of the women, Pamela, had been on numerous digs and was well schooled. With scientists Dr. João Cascalheira, Dr. Célia Gonçalves, Dr. Lino André, and several graduate students on-site, we were skillfully guided through our first day.

We were assigned our areas and moved down into the already-excavated area via steps cut out of the earth and with the help of a hand or two. The three walls in my corner were about shoulder height on me when I stood. Once again, it was kneel on the pad or sit on the dirt and scrape with our trowels, ever on the lookout for items that might be significant—in this case, bone, shells, charcoal, and stone of shapes that might be tools or stones larger than a small fist.

When our buckets were full, we took them to a shady spot under an oak-cork tree, the first I had ever seen. Someone had harvested part of the cork (the bark), so it was easy to see how thick the bark was. Otherwise, it certainly looked like an oak by the shape of the leaves and the little acorns. We picked up a set of round sieves (larger holes on top and finer ones underneath), poured some of the bucket's contents into the sieve, propped it on our knees, and began to poke through the material with our fingers. The graduate students helped us, and that way, we learned as they quickly spotted something—a sliver that looked like wood but was straight was a rabbit bone. It was so small I was hard-pressed to think what part of the rabbit it came from, or maybe rabbits were a lot smaller 4,000 years ago. Whole shells were put aside, and itty-bitty shells with round holes in them (ornaments) were set aside, too, as were bits of charcoal.

After we worked our way through the two layers of sieves, we dumped the remaining detritus and headed back with our empty buckets to start again. At lunchtime, we rode back to our home in the van; we were covered with dust and dirt. Back in my room, I discovered the mesh holes in the front of my sneakers I had worn had sifted the soil even further. My feet were coated in powdered dirt. Jane showed me how she clapped her dusty shoes out the window, and after I did that, I headed for the bathroom to clean my feet before lunch.

The lab where we would work was just down the street, and we walked there after lunch. Our worktables were outside under a roof. The work dealt with washing and sorting an even finer degree of sample. Magnifying glasses and headlamps were useful for this task. At

Opposite top: **Sometimes sifting is easier in a reclining position.** *Opposite bottom:* **This tool shows the size of the things for which we were looking. It is a type of geometric microlith—or minute, shaped flint—typically part of a composite tool such as a spear (courtesy Mary Rowe, Expedition Advisor, Earthwatch).**

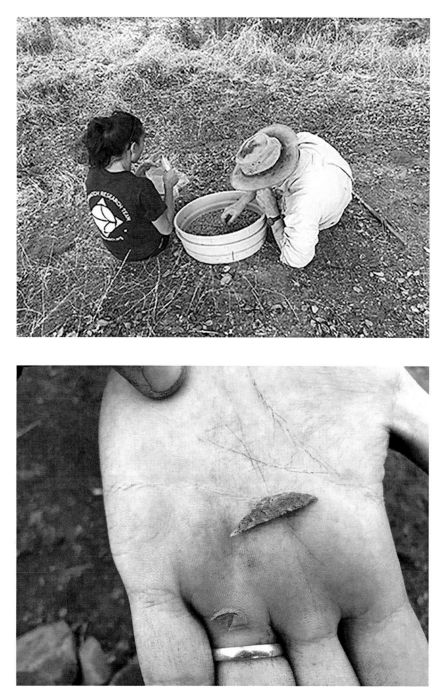

every step, just as I learned in Colorado, the findings were coded so that they could be mapped to the exact places in the earth where they were found. When we found a rock of the appropriate size at the dig, one of the students would use a laser to triangulate the position of the place it was found before we removed it.

After lab, we were free until dinner and could have a shower and really get that dirt off. During those late afternoons, some of us rambled about the area. There wasn't a lot to see, but whatever we saw was old. I visited a small grocery store and was delighted to see all kinds of chorizo apparently hand made locally. I really wanted to take some of that home but knew bringing meat into the country might be risky as it could be confiscated. In the end, with that as a deterrent, I told myself I didn't want to stink up my suitcase and possibly lose the sausage, too.

We often saw the countess out and about with her dogs. She had three different canines that followed her everywhere and set up a ruckus when they saw us. She was very friendly and invited us to use the swimming pool behind her section of the palace. I don't know if anyone did.

Our evening meals at the local restaurants were a lot of fun. All the scientists and students dined with us, and we got to know each other that way. Drs. Cascalheira and Gonçalves are not only fellow professionals but also married; they were expecting their first child rather soon. They promised to let us know about the baby, and we all received the e-mail with the news of a healthy baby girl some weeks later. We also received a scientific report based on the work. Although all the charts and data points were more than I was ready to understand, it was very nice to know the following: "2018 was the first Earthwatch expedition in Muge and was supported by 25 citizen scientists that worked hard across the 6-week field campaign, performing a great diversity of tasks, including excavation, sieving, artifact washing, sorting, and labeling, sediment flotation, among others. As a result of their effort we were able to excavate more than 3,370 liters of sediment, collect more than 9,000 artifacts, and piece plot with a total station more than 10,000 points."

I had once doubted the usefulness of my scientific work on a project—the one in South Africa with the meerkats. I expressed this doubt to Earthwatch and received an e-mail from the scientists assuring me the data I had collected was valuable to them. The sheer amount of data collected by all the teams in 2018 at the Portugal site was quite amazing to me. It looks like I had been a citizen scientist long before I had ever heard of the term—something that would not have happened had I not gone the route of volunteer vacations.

Epilogue:
Harvesting the Fruit
of the Travel Seeds

While I was volunteering, I also fit in some regular travel. There was the cruise in Tahiti with Wally. I went off on my own on a tour of Morocco, where I got to ride a camel in the Sahara and sleep under the stars. I went off on a trip to Bhutan in the Himalayas and, on the way back, added a short stopover in Paris, where I rented an apartment to find out what it was like to be on my own in a foreign country. It was quite nice, and, as I wandered from one landmark to another, I didn't mind getting lost at all. My friend Martha and I made a combined London-and-Paris trip and had a great time hitting all the thrift stores. Another time, I had a lovely sojourn to the Dordogne part of France to enjoy an embroidery workshop with an English artist. My brother and I scooted off to Ireland to see the land of our ancestors, only to find out we weren't Irish at all. I got a chance to see Sweden with friends who were staying there one summer. Martha and Thomas taught me the joys of *fika* (pronounced "feeka"), coffee and first-rate pastries.

I wanted to see the world, and I have seen a fair amount of it—the Himalayas, Brazilian jungles, ancient cities, and the Saharan Desert. I've been shown kindness from strangers whose language, religion, and very beings were as different from mine as I could imagine. The scientific programs I worked on were fascinating. And maybe, just maybe, I helped some people—rather briefly—who were suffering, and perhaps educated a few with English-speaking tips.

But the balance is way out of whack. I have thought, from the first volunteer trip I took, that I came back far richer by what I experienced

199

than the worth of anything I had done for others. It's like the decision to go into the Peace Corps that I made in college. I was looking at what I was going to get out of it. Any poke into the literature about why people volunteer will tell you that some do it to give back, and others do it to develop new skills or build their experience or knowledge. Obviously, I fall into the second camp. Then there is the unconscious volunteering I learned from my mother. Just do things, like pulling the weeds as I pass a walkway to a park and repairing the little free library near our home when the door won't close properly. These are just little things that need to be done. Calling the keepers of the library about the door or the town about the weeds—now that's too much trouble, as far as I'm concerned.

My memories of holding the twin baby boys in Romania, getting Vasula to smile from her wheelchair in Greece, and playing games with those hospitalized tots in Brazil—these things have become a part of me. Meeting these people and working with them has changed my perspective forever. They and the people who supported them in their countries have taught me about dignity, patience, and the great combination of suffering and joy that makes up life. And each and every time one of my soul souvenirs comes out and greets me, I am grateful that I packed my bag and went out there to get it. Those memories are invaluable payment for unpaid work. Pico Iyer said it best, "A person susceptible to 'wanderlust' is not so much addicted to movement as committed to transformation."

Heading for 80, I'm taking everything I've learned from these trips and going out into the rest of my life as a power *pani*.

Index

Numbers in *bold italics* indicate pages with illustrations

Index